ALBUM OF
AMERICAN HISTORY

RELATED WORKS

Atlas of American History

Dictionary of American Biography

Concise Dictionary of American Biography

Dictionary of American History

Concise Dictionary of American History

ALBUM OF AMERICAN HISTORY

SUPPLEMENT
1968 to 1982

NEW YORK

CHARLES SCRIBNER'S SONS

Copyright © 1985 Charles Scribner's Sons

Library of Congress Cataloging in Publication Data

Main entry under title:

Album of American history. Supplement, 1968–1982.

1. United States—History—Pictorial works.
I. Album of American History.
E178.5.A48   1981   973.92′022′2   82–42761
ISBN 0–684–17440–5

1 3 5 7 9 11 13 15 17 19   V/C   20 18 16 14 12 10 8 6 4 2

Printed in the United States of America.

ACKNOWLEDGMENTS

Joseph Abeles Studio

Air France

Alyeska Pipeline Service Company

Amblin Entertainment

American Automobile Association

American Broadcasting Company (ABC)

American Iron and Steel Institute

Archive Pictures, Inc.

Asheville (North Carolina) Area Chamber of Commerce

AT&T Corporate Archive

Automated Building Components, Inc.

Bethlehem Steel Corporation

The Bettmann Archive

Craig Brewer

British Broadcasting Corporation

Brookhaven National Laboratory

Buick Motor Division, General Motors Corporation

Cadillac Motor Car Division, General Motors Corporation

Camera Five

Woodfin Camp & Associates

Century Village West, Boca Raton, Fla.

Cessna Aircraft Corporation

Chevrolet Motor Division, General Motors Corporation

Chicago Transit Authority

Columbia Pictures

Consolidated Edison

Creative Time, Inc.

Charles Deaton

Diamond International

Walt Disney Productions

Drexel Heritage Furnishings, Inc.

Exxon Corporation

Florida Department of Commerce

GF Furniture Systems
The Goodyear Tire and Rubber Company
Gorchev & Gorchev Photography
The Grand Union Company

Harkness Ballet
Hawaii Visitors Bureau
Henson Associates, Inc.
Houston (Texas) Chamber of Commerce

Idaho State Historical Society

Jacob K. Javits Convention Center of New York
Jones and Laughlin Steel Corporation

Kansas State University
Knoxville (Tennessee) World's Fair
James J. Kriegsmann

Lautman
Library of Congress
London Weekend Television
Lucasfilm Ltd.

MCA, Inc.
McDonnell Douglas Corporation
McGraw-Hill Publications, Inc.
McIlhenny Co.
Magic Chef, Inc.
Magnum Photos, Inc.
Maine Department of Commerce and Industry
Louis Mélançon
Metro-Goldwyn-Mayer, Inc. (MGM)
Metropolitan Museum of Art, New York

Minneapolis Convention and Visitor Commission
Missouri Division of Tourism
William Morgan Architects

Nashville (Tennessee) Chamber of Commerce
National Aeronautics and Space Administration (NASA)
The National Archives
National Cotton Council of America
National Park Service
Nautilus Health Equipment
New York Cosmos
New York Public Library Picture Collection
New York State Office of General Services
New York Stock Exchange
North Dakota Tourism Promotion

Oklahoma Tourism and Recreation Department
Oregon State

Pan American World Airways
Paramount Pictures Corporation
I. M. Pei and Partners
Port Authority of New York and New Jersey
John Portman and Associates
Public Broadcasting System (PBS)

RCA Corporation
Reynolds Metals Company
Robert Yarnall Richie

San Diego Metropolitan Transit Development Board
San Francisco–Bay Area Rapid Transit (BART)
Sears, Roebuck, and Co.
A. O. Smith Harvestore Products, Inc.
Soil Conservation Service, United States Department of Agriculture
Ezra Stoller, ESTO Photographics, Inc.

Tandem Productions
Texas State Department of Highways—Travel and Information Division
20th Century-Fox Corporation

United Artists
United Press International (UPI)
United States Army
United States Army Information Office, West Point, New York
United States Army News Features
United States Coast Guard
United States Department of Agriculture
United States Department of Defense
United States Department of Housing and Urban Development
United States Peace Corps/Action
Universal Pictures

Vassar College
Vermont Development Corporation

Warner Bros.
Washington (D.C.) Convention and Visitors Association
Washington State Travel
Wayne Corporation
John Weber Gallery
Western Nuclear, Inc.
Westin Hotels
Wide World Photos
Burton Wilson
WIND SURF magazine
Wolfe & Associates, Inc.
Women's Wear Daily/Fairchild Syndicate
Wyoming Travel Commission

CONTENTS

INTRODUCTION

his Supplement to the *Album of American History* records the story of the people of the United States in pictures in the years between 1968 and 1982. As in the original volumes, the editors have adhered to the policy that the pictures present the history of the period while the text assumes the subordinate role of an explanatory narrative. The pictures portray both the diverse streams of American culture and the common threads that hold Americans together, concentrating on the many elements of daily life rather than on journalistic events. Each picture has been carefully selected to provide a representative view of the period covered.

In the mid-1960s, America seemed increasingly fragmented, not only by class and race but also philosophically and morally. Special-interest groups proliferated, and the melting-pot theory of America degenerated as ethnic awareness flourished. Widely disparate visions of America's future arose between those who believed in laissez-faire capitalism and those who preferred more government controls, between those who favored higher industrialization and those who wanted a more pastoral future, and between those whose dream was American materialism and those who reacted against the impersonality of suburbia and mass marketing. With the "baby boom" generation's coming of age, a revolution in American manners and mores occurred that seemed counter to traditional values, and the widening involvement in Vietnam created a growing division between supporters and opponents of that war that at times seemed to be tearing the nation apart.

American space technology came of age with the moon landing in 1969, which brought scientific advances that affected daily life from clothing to cookware. Computers became available to the wider public, medicine was transformed by advances in genetic research, and practical applications were made of the laser and microwaves and the new more durable plastics and metals. But if scientific technology seemed to expand the American material domain, its growth was accompanied by a new awareness of the limited capacities of nature, brought home by shortages in fuels and industrial metals. The recession of 1972–1974, the inability of American technology to overcome the ills of poverty, and the growing political scandals culminating in Watergate caused many to become disenchanted with the American dream.

A constitutional crisis was averted in 1974 with the resignation of President Richard Nixon, and the following years saw a painful recovery of confidence in the American system culminating in the 1976 exuberant Bicentennial celebration of independence. A diversified nation looked toward an unpredictable future: a technological revolution was transforming the manner in which Americans conducted their business and lives; a sexual revolution was affecting the American family structure; and a communications revolution was changing the dispersal of knowledge. There was no greater example of the power of the electronic media than in the election of 1976. At the same time there was an underlying reaction to rapid change, exemplified by a growing interest in the occult, mysticism, and self-improvement movements. Indeed, a seeming preoccupation with self gave rise to what became known as the "me generation."

By the late 1970s many Americans felt that the permissiveness of the 1960s was at the root of the violence that seemed to permeate American culture, in literature, films, television, music, and even fashion. Some saw the Iranian crisis and the Jonestown mass suicides as a failure of the American spirit. Others blamed spiraling inflation and the impersonality of American culture. A growing religious revivalism attracted many Americans with its reaffirmation of traditional values, as did the election of Ronald Reagan as president in 1980. As the United States entered the 1980s, it was beset by growing economic problems and rising unemployment. But, as in the past, America remained a land of many contrasts, of timelessness and rapid change, and unexplored possibilities.

The Editors

1.

THE PRESIDENCY

Change, scandal, and controversy marked the presidency from 1968 to 1982. The incumbent, Democrat Lyndon Johnson, chose not to seek reelection in 1968. His Republican successor was Richard M. Nixon, who had been vice-president during the two terms of Dwight D. Eisenhower, 1953–1961, and who had narrowly lost a bid for the presidency to John F. Kennedy in 1960. As president, Nixon made significant advances in foreign policy, notably in ending American involvement in the Vietnam War, renewing arms-control negotiations with the USSR, and officially recognizing the Communist government of mainland China (*see* Chapter 2). Domestically, Nixon reversed many of the Kennedy-Johnson social and economic programs, impounded funds for social programs, vetoed social legislation, and presided over a major recession. Nixon's second term was largely devoted to dealing with scandal. His vice-president, Spiro Agnew, resigned in the face of criminal charges and was replaced by Gerald Ford. Nixon himself was impeached for alleged criminal acts in what was known as the Watergate Affair, and resigned in 1974 to avoid trial by the Senate. (The only other president to be impeached was Andrew Johnson, whose trial in 1868 did not result in conviction.) The presidency was assumed by Gerald Ford, who was the subject of two unsuccessful assassination attempts in his two years in office. Ford had attained the two highest offices in the land because of resignations for alleged crimes, but he was unable to gain reelection on his own, losing in 1976 to Democrat Jimmy (James Earl) Carter. The Carter presidency was marked by a major achievement—a peace agreement in the Middle East—but ended in apparent humiliation in failing to free American hostages seized along with our embassy in Iran. Carter was defeated in a landslide by Republican Ronald Reagan in 1980. By far the most conservative president in at least fifty years, Reagan was wounded in an assassination attempt, but quickly recovered. In 1984 he won reelection, again in a landslide, over Walter Mondale, who had been Carter's vice-president. Seldom in the history of the country had the presidency seen such turmoil.

Lyndon Baines Johnson, who had assumed the presidency following the assassination of John F. Kennedy, was elected to a full term in 1964. Two major developments marked his presidency. One was enactment of the greatest body of social legislation—Johnson's "Great Society" program—since the days of his mentor, Franklin D. Roosevelt. The other was escalation of American involvement in the Vietnam War to its maximum (*see* Chapter 2; *see also* Volume VI, Chapters 2 and 3). Midway through his term of office, the financial costs and the toll in dead and wounded turned public opinion against the war, and against both Johnson himself and his domestic programs. On March 31, 1968, he made public two decisions which he hoped would heal the national dissension over the war and social welfare. He is shown (*page 4*) preparing for the television broadcast in which he announced major deescalation of the Vietnam War. He went on to astonish the country by announcing that he would not seek a second term as president. This unexpected news

opened the Democratic party candidacy to three men: Vice-President Hubert H. Humphrey, Johnson's choice as his successor; Senator Eugene McCarthy; and Senator Robert F. Kennedy, the former attorney general.

President Johnson's domestic achievements began in 1964 with passage of the most sweeping civil rights legislation in American history. His Great Society program included Medicaid and Medicare assistance for the poor and elderly; the Office of Economic Opportunity; the Equal Employment Opportunity Commission; Volunteers in Service to America (VISTA), a kind of domestic Peace Corps to work in depressed areas; the Job Corps, which created work for the hard-core unemployed; Head Start programs to help prepare culturally and economically deprived children for school; two new cabinet positions: the Department of Housing and Urban Development, and the Department of Transportation; and many more programs and agencies (*see* Volume VI, Chapter 4).

Although Johnson accomplished much of what John Kennedy had proposed and went on to achieve a great deal more, bitterness and opposition arose from several sources. Conservative Americans were strongly against legislating social change, especially on Johnson's sweeping scale. The poor suffered from unfulfilled assistance and the middle class from increased taxation, both from the economy's inability to simultaneously support a war effort and extensive social welfare. Young men in increasing numbers resisted having to fight in a war that seemed more and more futile, mismanaged, and immoral. The growing wave of protest attacked all government activity, as shown by the structures (*page 5*) erected during a demonstration in a national park.

Photo by Jack Rottier, *courtesy*, National Park Service

THE DEMOCRATS

Senator Eugene McCarthy of Minnesota, whose main issue was withdrawal from the Vietnam War, showed himself a strong candidate by almost winning the New Hampshire primary (March 12, 1968) against President Johnson. After Johnson withdrew and Robert F. Kennedy entered the Democratic contest, McCarthy's success was limited.

UPI/Bettmann

UPI/Bettmann

Senator Robert F. Kennedy of New York, after winning the California Democratic presidential primary election, in Los Angeles, May 11, 1968. A few minutes after this photograph was taken he was assassinated by Sirhan B. Sirhan. Kennedy's death made the nomination of Hubert Humphrey almost inevitable.

CHICAGO, 1968

The 1968 Democratic party convention was a disaster, marked by riots and civil rights protests outside, and by dissension and bickering within. Although highly regarded for his record, vice-president Hubert H. Humphrey (left) was accused by the left wing of the party of favoring the establishment. However, his rivals, Eugene McCarthy and George McGovern, had limited support, and Humphrey received the presidential nomination. Senator Edmund Muskie of Maine (right) was nominated for vice-president.

AP/Wide World Photos

A bitter convention quarrel about credentials ended, for Georgia at least, with a compromise on August 27, 1968. Half the state's seats were awarded to the regular delegates and the other half to a biracial group headed by Julian Bond, seen next to his state's placard.

In addition to questions of racial balance, delegate seating was contested on issues of women's rights and political orientation. The schism created by these and other disputes caused a large portion of the voters to sit out the election in November. At the convention, after party problems were resolved—to the dissatisfaction of many—the delegates paid tribute to the memory of Robert F. Kennedy.

PROTEST—THE YIPPIES

AP/Wide World Photos

When it became obvious that the Democratic party convention would not follow the wishes or plans of the leftists, Jerry Rubin and his associates formed the Youth International Party, or Yippies, to disrupt the proceedings. For a short time before violence erupted, the Yippies ran a pig as a mock candidate for the presidential nomination.

Yippies and other demonstrators were determined to get to the convention site through police lines. In what was afterward described as a police riot they were first repulsed bodily and with clubs; as the violence escalated, tear gas and rifle butts were used.

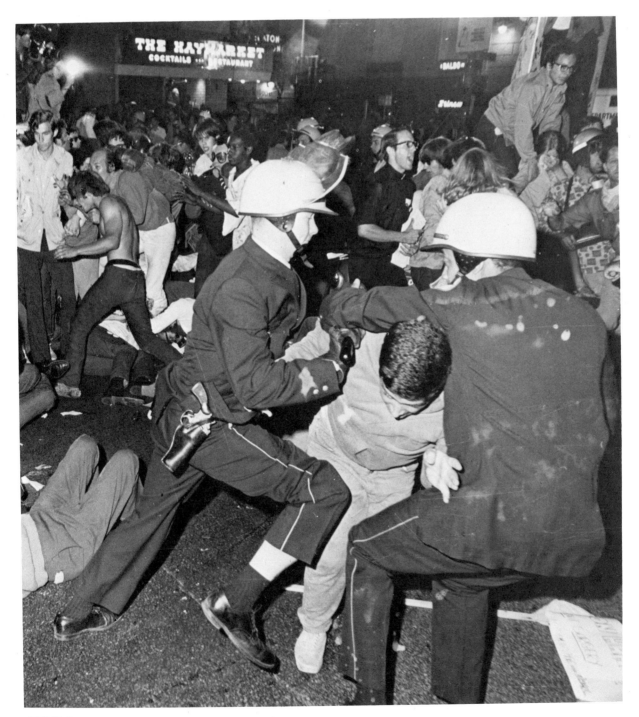

UPI/Bettmann

PROTEST—THE CHICAGO SEVEN

During the September 1969 trial of the Chicago Seven—protesters charged with inciting riot during the Democratic convention—Lee Weiner and Abbie Hoffman (right) clown by wrapping themselves in white paper barber's gowns while a friend prepares to clip off a lock of hair to send to codefendant Jerry Rubin, then in Cook County jail. The gesture mocked the prosecution's characterization of the seven as "long-haired hippies."

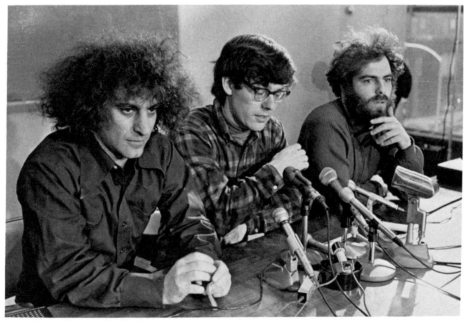

Three of the Chicago Seven defendants (left to right), Abbie Hoffman, Rennie Davis, and Jerry Rubin, hold a press conference February 14, 1970, while waiting for the jury to render its verdict. Five of the seven were found guilty of crossing a state line to incite riot.

Having defeated the Democrats in 1968, Richard M. Nixon (right) and Spiro T. Agnew were renominated for the presidency and vice-presidency at the Republican party convention in Miami Beach, Florida, on August 23, 1972. They defeated Democrats George McGovern and Sargent Shriver in the November election.

Less than a year after reelection, Spiro T. Agnew resigned the vice-presidency in Baltimore, Maryland, on October 10, 1973, in return for a lenient sentence after pleading *nolo contendere* in a Justice Department investigation of alleged corrupt practices and income tax evasion. He was succeeded by Representative Gerald R. Ford of Michigan, who later became president as a result of the Watergate scandal.

UPI/Bettmann

THE WATERGATE AFFAIR

AP/Wide World Photos

The Watergate office-apartment complex, near the Potomac River in Washington, D.C. On June 17, 1972, five men were arrested while trying to plant listening devices in the Democratic National Committee headquarters here, which began a series of events culminating in the resignation of President Richard Nixon.

G. Gordon Liddy, much the most colorful of the seven men arrested and convicted (January 1973) for the Watergate break-in, arrives at the Federal Correctional Institution at Danbury, Connecticut, to begin his six and one-half to twenty-year sentence for the crime. James McCord, another of those convicted, charged that there had been a cover-up to protect cabinet officials and White House staff.

AP/Wide World Photos

Cover-up charges were investigated by the Senate Watergate Committee, headed by Senator Sam Ervin (seated). Committee members and staff included (left to right) Senator Howard Baker, Tennessee; Senator Edward Gurney, Florida; H. William Shure, assistant minority counsel; Rufus Edmisten, deputy chief counsel; Senator Joseph Montoya, New Mexico; and Sam Dash, chief counsel. They are conferring about presidential aide J. R. Haldeman's invoking executive privilege in refusing to discuss tape recordings of conversations held in the Oval Office of the White House.

UPI/Bettmann

John W. Dean III, former White House counsel, appearing before the Senate Watergate Committee on June 29, 1972. Dean testified that he had warned President Nixon that the case against the seven men charged with the Watergate break-in could not be "contained" indefinitely. Behind him sits his wife, Maureen.

UPI/Bettmann

AP/Wide World Photos

E. Howard Hunt, former CIA agent and convicted Watergate conspirator, testifies before the Senate committee on September 24, 1973.

H. R. Haldeman, one of two top aides forced to resign in President Nixon's efforts to deflect suspicion in the Watergate cover-up, testifies before the Senate committee on July 31, 1973.

AP/Wide World Photos

John Erlichman, the second Nixon aide to resign, refusing to answer press questions after arraignment for burglary, perjury, and conspiracy in a break-in at the California office of Daniel Ellsberg's psychiatrist. Ellsberg was a key figure in the Pentagon Papers case, which revealed questionable government actions in the Vietnam War (see Chapter 2).

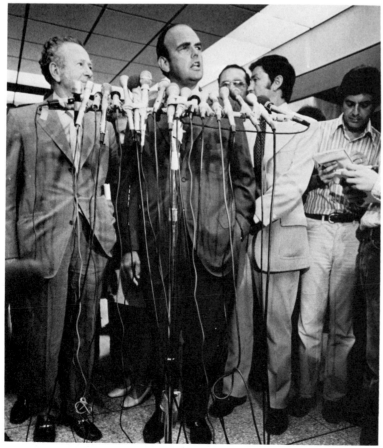

AP/Wide World Photos

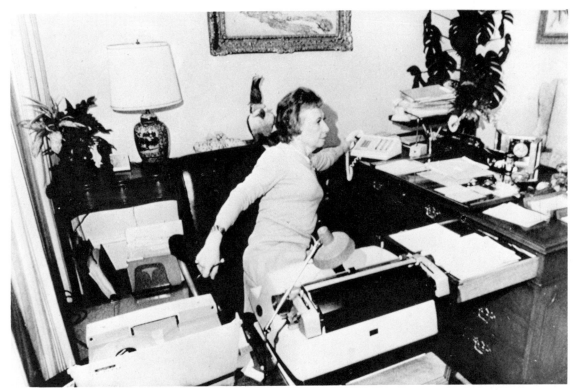

UPI/Bettmann

Tapes of secretly recorded presidential conversations were crucial evidence in the Watergate cover-up investigation. Rose Mary Woods, President Nixon's personal secretary, testified in U. S. District Court on November 23, 1973, that she had no idea how eighteen minutes of material were erased from a June 20 tape.

U. S. District Judge John Sirica ordered the White House to deliver sixty-four subpoenaed tapes to Special Prosecutor Leon Jaworski, who had replaced Archibald Cox, dismissed by President Nixon for demanding tapes. Upheld by the Supreme Court, this was the final critical ruling in unraveling the Watergate cover-up.

AP/Wide World Photos

UPI/Bettmann

There were growing indications that the president himself was involved in the Watergate cover-up. The House of Representatives instructed its Judiciary Committee to conduct an investigation. Committee chairman Peter Rodino of New Jersey (with gavel) presided over televised hearings that fascinated and agonized the country. In six days of hearings, July 24–30, 1973, the evidence became convincing for more than two-thirds of the thirty-eight-member committee. The full House voted 412 to 3 to accept the committee report, including a bill of impeachment for three crimes: criminal conspiracy to obstruct justice, abuses of power that constituted failure to carry out the presidential oath of office, and unconstitutional defiance of subpoenas from the House of Representatives. It was the first presidential impeachment in more than a century, and only the second in the country's history.

THE END OF A PRESIDENCY

In the East Room of the White House, August 9, 1974, President Richard Milhous Nixon announces his resignation from office. The first president to do so, he thus avoided Senate impeachment proceedings.

A NEW PRESIDENT

The vice-president succeeded to the vacated office. One of Gerald R. Ford's first acts as president was to grant a full pardon to Richard Nixon for all federal crimes he "committed or may have committed or taken part in" while in office. Ford's action, considered of doubtful legality by some jurists, touched off much public dispute. "He has suffered enough" was set against "It was all prearranged."

On September 5, 1975, Lynette Alice (Squeaky) Fromme was seized as she pointed a .45-caliber pistol at President Gerald Ford in Sacramento, California. Here she arrives at the Federal Building from jail several days later, seeking a reduction in her $1-million bail. On September 22, Sara Jane Moore was arrested in San Francisco just after firing a .38-caliber pistol at the President; the shot was deflected. Both women were convicted of attempted assassination.

UPI/Bettmann

THE 1976 CAMPAIGN

UPI/Bettmann

Before the 1976 presidential primaries, reforms in delegate selection changed the concept of the election. Candidates now worked anxiously to gather as many primary delegates as possible before the party convention. Here President Ford addresses a crowd in Lansing, Michigan, on May 13, 1976.

AP/Wide World Photos

Unsuccessful 1976 Republican primary candidate Ronald Reagan is shown here in Houston, Texas, supported by fellow motion picture actors (left to right) Lloyd Nolan, Efrem Zimbalist, Jr., and James Stewart.

AP/Wide World Photos

Governor Jimmy Carter of Georgia, with Senator Birch Bayh of Indiana, greets a well-wisher at an Indianapolis Western Electric plant, May 5, 1976. Bayh had just withdrawn from the Democratic primary race to endorse Carter.

AP/Wide World Photos

Unsuccessful Democratic primary contender Governor Edmund G. Brown, Jr., of California tries to capture a vote in Warwick, Rhode Island, as Mrs. Jimmy Carter looks on.

UPI/Bettmann

The second debate in the presidential campaign between the Democratic nominee, Jimmy Carter, and Republican Gerald Ford, held October 6, 1976, in San Francisco.

On January 20, 1977, James Earl Carter, Jr., was sworn in as the thirty-ninth president of the United States. Following the ceremony, the Carters broke tradition by walking the mile and a half from the Capitol building to the White House.

Ronald Reagan during a Columbia, South Carolina, debate with George Bush, John Connally, and Howard Baker for the Republican 1980 nomination for president.

AP/Wide World Photos

UPI/Bettmann

Candidate Ronald Reagan at a $1,000-a-plate fund-raising dinner in New York, September 1980. Frank Sinatra is at his right. Nineteen such affairs held across the country helped his successful bid for the presidency.

UPI/Bettmann

This photograph was taken March 30, 1981, in Washington, just after
the attempted assassination of President Reagan by John Hinckley.
Presidential Press Secretary James Brady, who was also shot and suffered severe brain damage, lies on the sidewalk at right center, next to a
wounded policeman. Hinckley is buried in the group of police and Secret
Service agents holding him in the background. Hinckley's trial turned
out to be controversial when the jury held him not responsible for his
actions because of insanity.

PRESIDENTIAL DEATHS

As the 1960s gave way to the 1970s, three ex-presidents died within four years. In the picture *below*, crews stand ready for a twenty-one-gun salute at the funeral of Harry Truman. This scene is at the Truman Library in Independence, Missouri, where the funeral was held two days after his death on December 26, 1972. Dwight D. Eisenhower had died on March 28, 1969, after several heart attacks. Lyndon B. Johnson died on January 23, 1973, less than a month after Truman. He was buried at his home, the LBJ Ranch, in Texas.

Courtesy, U. S. Army

2.

VIETNAM AND FOREIGN POLICY

The first United States troops had been sent to Vietnam in 1961 by John F. Kennedy, during the initial year of his presidency. In response to a North Vietnamese attack on American destroyers in the Gulf of Tonkin, Congress passed a War Powers Act that authorized President Lyndon Johnson to send additional troops and to take whatever other military action he and the Joint Chiefs of Staff thought necessary. By 1966 there were 190,000 American troops in Vietnam, and some 550,000 three years later, heavily supported by air power. The soaring costs of the war alarmed Congress, which cut back spending on domestic programs, both to restrain the president and to ensure continued military funding. Congress also demanded evidence of satisfactory progress in the war. This led to inaccurate and overly optimistic intelligence reports, and to misleading if not outright false reports of the number of enemy soldiers killed, territory taken, and strategic sites bombed. The extent of the inaccuracies and mismanagement of the campaign were revealed by the so-called Pentagon Papers, published in 1971 (see page 41). Here, General William Westmoreland, commander in chief of American forces in Vietnam, briefs Senator Richard Russell, Chairman of the Senate Armed Services Committee, in November 1967.

Courtesy, U. S. Department of Defense

United States marines in Hue, midway between north and south Vietnam, February 1968. The war-shattered tower in the background marked one of the gates to the ancient city.

AP/Wide World Photos

Members of the U. S. 1st Cavalry Division attack an enemy position at Lang Vei, April 19, 1968.

Photo by P. J. Griffiths, © 1969 Magnum Photos, from *Crisis in America*, published by Ridge Press and Holt, Rinehart & Winston

Near Saigon, October 1968.

AP/Wide World Photos

United States marines land in the hills near the former U. S. base at Khe Sanh, October 1968.

Courtesy, U. S. Department of Defense

U. S. marines on patrol. Jungle fighting and guerrilla tactics severely tested American military strategy.

ANTIWAR PROTEST

In protest against the draft and the Vietnam War, a young man burns his registration card during Stop the Draft Week, October 16–20, 1967. Note the peace symbols that he and the onlooker wear.

UPI/Bettmann

United States marshals remove a peace demonstrator from an entrance to the Pentagon, October 22, 1967.

AP/Wide World Photos

AP/Wide World Photos

The Rev. Philip F. Berrigan (center) and his brother, Father Daniel Berrigan, members of the group that came to be known as the Harrisburg Eight, were Catholic priests well known for their antiwar activities. Here they have set fire to records taken from a local draft board in Baltimore, May 17, 1968. Both men received prison sentences.

On April 9, 1969, Harvard students demanding the abolition of ROTC programs at the university seized the administration building. They are seen here urging fellow students to vote against on-campus military training.

AP/Wide World Photos

At Kent State University, Ohio, panicky National Guardsmen fired into a crowd and killed four students during an antiwar demonstration on May 5, 1970. The shooting took place near the building at the upper left. In the foreground is the ROTC building burned out by the demonstrators. (*Below*) Soldiers, behind the rope in the background, use tear gas against Kent State protesters.

AP/Wide World Photos

There was a blue-collar backlash against the antiwar movement. Mayor
John Lindsay of New York had ordered the flag to be flown at half-staff
on May 11, 1970, in memory of the students killed at Kent State. About
two thousand workers responded by marching around City Hall shout-
ing, "U.S.A. all the way!" and "Lindsay must go!"

In a "spring offensive" against the
Vietnam War, members of pro-
testing groups assemble at the
Capitol on May 5, 1971.

UPI/Bettmann

Photo by Dick Frear, *courtesy*, National Park Service

On January 12, 1972, the first anniversary of the indictment of the Harrisburg Eight, a clash occurred between antiwar and prowar groups on the steps of Independence Hall, Philadelphia.

SIGNS OF PATRIOTISM

Despite the antiwar movement, enlistment rates were up. Here, at Parris Island, South Carolina, a Marine drill sergeant instructs recruits on barracks regulations.

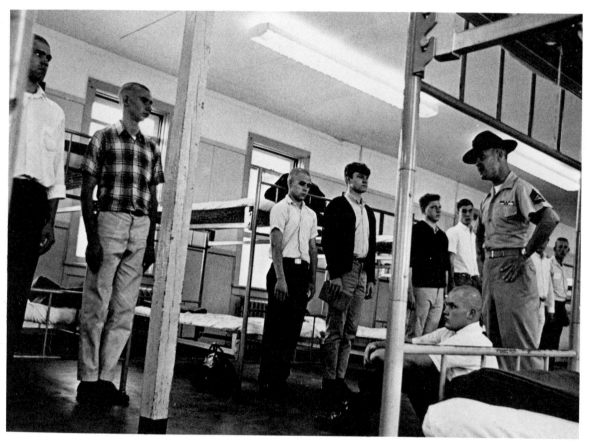

Courtesy, U. S. Department of Defense

This parody of James Montgomery Flagg's famous World War I poster (in which Uncle Sam sternly said, "I Want You!") is typical of those circulated among draft-age men in the Vietnam War era.

The new look in recruitment posters stressed macho images rather than the "fun, travel, and adventure" approach used prior to Vietnam.

Courtesy, U. S. Army

THE BEGINNING OF THE END

UPI/Bettmann

The Department of Justice was unable to prevent publication of the so-called Pentagon Papers, a series of articles on the history of American involvement in the Vietnam War, which began running in the *New York Times* on June 13, 1971. Based on a top secret study prepared for Secretary of Defense Robert McNamara by the Rand Corporation, the articles revealed bungling and deception. It was soon discovered that the documents had been turned over to the press by Dr. Daniel Ellsberg, who had helped prepare them for Rand. Here Ellsberg is addressing a press conference in Los Angeles on July 26, 1972.

UPI/Bettmann

In January 1973 the warring parties in Vietnam reached a peace agreement, and a cease-fire took effect. A great many American ground troops had previously been withdrawn in favor of a stepped-up air war; now most of the remaining ground forces left.

The South Vietnam government of Nguyen Van Thieu, shown here (right) reviewing troops shortly before being elected president in 1967, lasted twenty-eight months after the 1973 cease-fire peace agreement was signed. Former premier Nguyen Cao Ky (dark uniform), who had been vice-president from 1967 to 1971, fled to the United States at the end. He now resides in California.

Photo by Marilyn Silverstone, Magnum

VIETNAM: THE END

AP/Wide World Photos

Claiming repeated peace violations as justification, Communist North Vietnamese forces invaded the south in January 1975, creating panic and quickly toppling the Thieu government. Here U. S. Marines are landing at the American Embassy compound in Saigon in an attempt to restore order and evacuate the remaining U. S. personnel. South Vietnam surrendered the next day, April 30, 1975.

UPI/Bettmann

In the aftermath of surrender, great numbers of Vietnamese "boat people" fled by sea in craft of all sizes. Some 2,700 are here crowded on a freighter that reached Manila Bay. The United States resettled many boat people, who generally were welcomed but in some instances met racial prejudice and violence.

FOREIGN POLICY

America's international role became increasingly varied and complex in the 1970s, especially after involvement in Indochina ended. Improving relations with the U.S.S.R. were adversely affected by recognition of the government of mainland China, a development that astonished many in the United States because it was achieved by a Republican president, Richard Nixon, who had built a political career on anti-Communism. During the term of Democratic president Jimmy Carter, from 1976 to 1980, major accomplishments were made in Central America and in the Middle East, both areas that were to become of extreme concern in the 1980s.

UPI/Bettmann

In October 1972, President Richard Nixon met with Soviet Foreign Minister Andrei Gromyko to discuss possible troop reductions in Europe. Left to right: Soviet ambassador Anatoly Dobrynin, Gromyko, Nixon, Secretary of State William P. Rogers, presidential adviser Henry Kissinger.

UPI/Bettmann

Following the normalization of relations between the United States and the People's Republic of China, President and Mrs. Nixon visited a well-preserved portion of the Great Wall, near Peking, on December 21, 1972.

AP/Wide World Photos

The Panama Canal became an emotional issue in the late 1970s. In the treaty of 1904, Panama had ceded the Canal Zone to the United States in perpetuity, subject to a small yearly rental. This treaty had long been considered improper by the Panamanians, and in 1977 presidents Jimmy Carter (left) and Torrijos Herrera (right) agreed to a new treaty, under which the United States would gradually relinquish control of the canal to Panama by 1999. Although the American military establishment and conservative politicians were strongly opposed to the new treaty, it was ratified by the U. S. Senate in 1978.

The Panama Canal is of major economic and defense concern to the United States. Here, the 108-foot-wide battleship *New Jersey* barely squeezes into the 110-foot lock chambers of the canal.

At Camp David, Maryland, in September 1978, a solution was worked out to some problems in the Middle East. Premier Menachem Begin of Israel (left), President Carter, and President Anwar Sadat of Egypt agreed to defuse explosive issues. Egypt would institute normal relations with Israel and open the Suez Canal to international shipping; Israel would withdraw from occupied Egyptian territory in the Sinai and halt settlements in the Palestinian West Bank area of the Jordan River. It seemed a triumph for American diplomacy, and "the spirit of Camp David" became a rallying cry in later negotiations, but attempts to resolve the Palestinian question remain as bitter and frustrating as ever.

3.

BUSINESS, INDUSTRY, AND AGRICULTURE

The 1970s took business and manufacturing into the postindustrial age, an era in which communication, planning, management, and operations are controlled electronically at every level. Computers, already well established in the administration of large-scale operations, began to take over the day-to-day functioning of small as well as large businesses. By the early 1980s, individual computer terminals were replacing typewriters and teletype machines in offices of every kind. Supermarkets installed laser-beam readers at checkout counters that were interconnected with price-and-inventory computers that controlled individual cash registers in the store and warehouse operations miles away. Industry learned a painful lesson from foreign competition that computer-controlled robots were essential for modern manufacturing. American agriculture maintained its position as the most efficient food producer in the world, but learned again that business recession and foreign policy considerations could mean restricted profits even in seasons of great abundance.

By 1978, the trading floor of the New York Stock Exchange (*below*) was thoroughly equipped with video display units and computer input terminals, as were the offices of all major stockbrokers. A few years later, operations were totally electronic—in the "back room" where transactions were recorded and processed, as well as on the floor.

Photo by Edward C. Topple, New York Stock Exchange

Courtesy, AT&T Corporate Archive

Lines of desks equipped with card files and telephones, such as this A. T. & T. regional customer service office, gave way to modular offices (*below*) and computer work stations equipped with video displays, keyboards, and integrated voice communications.

Courtesy, GF Furniture Systems

Modular-design panels, desks, and storage units make it easy to create individual private work areas without permanent construction. An entire floor can be rearranged for any business purpose in a matter of hours.

UPI/Bettmann

While clerical businesses modernized, many small industries persisted in old practices as they tried to make a profit in the face of soaring costs and increasingly stiff competition. In New York's garment district, the facilities might be a bit better than the sweatshops of fifty years ago, but the exploitation of workers was little different among marginal business operators. Happy to have any sort of job, few foreign-born workers would protest if they received unfair wages or were deprived of benefits.

SMOKESTACK INDUSTRIES: STEEL

The American steel industry was slow to modernize; as a result, the mid-1970s recession caused many plants to reduce production severely or close down entirely. Modern, high-production facilities such as this basic oxygen furnace at the Lackawanna, New York, plant of Bethlehem Steel could not satisfy domestic demand, which opened the door to foreign steel produced at lower cost.

Courtesy, Bethlehem Steel Corporation

Courtesy, Bethlehem Steel Corporation

So-called submarine cars like this have a capacity of 330 tons of molten steel, more than two and a half times greater than that of old-style cars shown above. Lined with refractory ceramic, they transport molten metal from a blast furnace to shaping and forming machines at the plant in Sparrows Point, Maryland.

At the Hennepin Works of Jones & Laughlin Steel Corporation, in Pittsburgh, a five-stand cold reducing mill is operated from a control "pulpit" by one man. A computer program controls the actual functioning of the equipment. Such installations are essential in modern steel-making throughout the world.

Photo by Scott-d'Arazien, Inc., *courtesy,* Jones & Laughlin Steel Corp.

Video monitoring of production processes from a central control point has become standard in many industries. Here, engineers watch each step of wood chip handling and processing at the Old Town, Maine, plant of Diamond Corporation.

Courtesy, Diamond International

Aluminum manufacture requires vast amounts of electricity to produce twelve-ton ingots such as these being stacked at a Reynolds plant in McCook, Illinois. Production on this scale is a far cry from the early nineteenth century, when the difficulty of extraction made aluminum almost a precious metal: the Tsar of Russia had an aluminum crown among his treasures.

Courtesy, Reynolds Metals Co.

Courtesy, The Goodyear Tire & Rubber Co.

Automobile manufacture is a nationwide industry in the United States. While chassis production is still largely centered in the Midwest, automobile components are manufactured in almost every industrial state, and assembly plants are located throughout the country. This line of vulcanization molds for truck tires is in the Goodyear plant in Los Angeles.

Installing the power train in the chassis of what will be a new Cadillac, in the mid-1960s. While American companies maintained labor-intensive assembly lines through the 1980s, foreign manufacturers—especially the Japanese—converted to automation and robots. As a result, they cut heavily into car sales in the United States. Only in the 1980s did American manufacturers begin to change equipment and methods radically, a process complicated by union demands for job protection.

Courtesy, Cadillac Motor Car Division, General Motors Corp.

Courtesy, Cadillac Motor Car Division, General Motors Corp.

The license plate, LAST, marks the end of domestic production of convertibles, April 21, 1976. This is a Cadillac Eldorado. The passing of the convertible was widely mourned, but unnecessarily so. America's love for the fold-down top was too strong, and some companies resumed producing such models in the 1980s.

A growing concern for ecological balance brought most industrial operations under increasing scrutiny and criticism in the 1970s. Surface mining is very controversial because it strips away the covering layer and leaves the contours of an area permanently changed. In some cases a worked-over section can be filled and replanted, but that is not possible when vast amounts of ore-bearing earth must be removed and processed to obtain a relatively small amount of a final product such as uranium. This is the Day-Loma uranium mining complex in Wyoming. The main pit is 370 feet deep, and more than 23 million cubic yards of earth and stone have been removed.

Courtesy, Western Nuclear, Inc.

Courtesy, North Dakota Tourism Promotion

In the strip mining of coal, huge digging wheels like this proceed slowly across the side of a hill or mountain, leaving wide, barren, terrace-like ledges in their wake. Such operations now must meet government standards for environmental protection. Replanting is required as a means of erosion control.

The earth-moving vehicles used in large-scale highway, construction, and mining projects are bigger than many houses. This Unit Rig dump truck can carry a 200-ton load. Each of its six tires is almost twelve feet in diameter and weighs three and a half tons.

Courtesy, The Goodyear Tire & Rubber Co.

Modern materials cut the time and expense of all kinds of industrial and construction operations. Hoses that stand up to the constant abrasion of pumped concrete mix make it possible to pour footings and lay slabs in hours —jobs that took days when the material was moved by wheelbarrows or dump-buckets.

Courtesy, The Goodyear Tire & Rubber Co.

Some huge equipment is designed for precision work with the tiniest possible bits of material. Particle accelerators such as these at the Brookhaven National Laboratory, Upton, New York, are indispensable for the study of subatomic particles.

Courtesy, Brookhaven National Laboratory

LIVING OFF THE LAND

Courtesy, National Archives

Although commercial food production is highly mechanized in the United States, some crops require hand cultivation, especially in the early stages of growth. In such fields, the worker with a hoe is as essential as he has been for centuries. Little has changed, except perhaps for the clothing worn and the advent of steel-bladed tools. Many more crops require manual labor at harvest time (see page 69).

Courtesy, National Cotton Council

Once entirely achieved with manual labor—first with slaves, then with sharecroppers and migrant workers—commercial cotton production is today one of the most mechanized agricultural operations in America. When the crop is ready, three-wheel harvesters (*above*) proceed down the rows, stripping off the ripe bolls. Trucked in multi-ton loads to processing stations (*opposite, above*), the bolls are fed from overhead hoppers into giant gins that strip the cotton fibers from the seeds, hulls, and stalks of the plants.

Courtesy, National Cotton Council

Courtesy, The Goodyear Tire & Rubber Co.

Mass food production demands efficient methods for tending hundreds or even thousands of acres of a single crop. The self-propelled sprinkler shown *left* overcomes the inflexibility and limitations of fixed-pipe irrigation systems. It can deliver up to two and a half inches of "rain" over a ten-acre area in twenty-four hours. Most of the plants pressed down by the water supply hose spring back within a day.

UPI/Bettmann

Crop dusting from small airplanes can deliver insecticides or fertilizer where mobile equipment would damage the crop. In addition, a single plane needs only an hour or two to treat an area that would take a day or more using several spray trucks. This plane is dusting a California almond grove to help control a 1981 outbreak of Mediterranean fruit fly infestation.

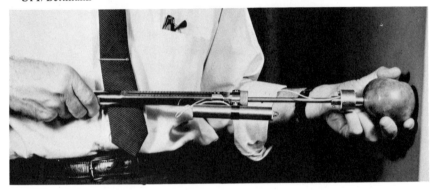

Courtesy, U. S. Department of Agriculture

(*Above*) Scientifically derived equipment is as important in modern agriculture as up-to-date research information. This kind of apple tester originated in the laboratory but is now a standard commercial device. It depresses the flesh of the fruit about 5/100 inch; the resistance, shown on the pressure scale, indicates the degree of ripeness. This is valuable because many modern varieties of apples reach a mature color long before they are fully ripe.

(*Right*) Genetic research has found new methods of producing hybrids with longer life, increased output, greater resistance to disease, and other desirable characteristics. A technique called parasexual hybridization fuses genetic material from two different species to produce cells with entirely new characteristics. These research biologists at Brookhaven National Laboratory are examining early results of the procedure in 1972. The technique advanced greatly in the succeeding decade.

Courtesy, Brookhaven National Laboratory

Courtesy, A. O. Smith Harvestore Products, Inc.

Steadily rising prices for seed, fertilizer, animal feed, equipment, and fuel made it increasingly difficult for the small-scale farmer to show a profit. Improved equipment and new information from agricultural extension services were potentially helpful, but rising interest rates made it impossible for many to borrow the money needed to improve their operations. Federal support money went disproportionately to the largest, industrialized food producers. By the early 1980s, small-farm bankruptcies, foreclosures, and sales to land developers had reached a new high.

The farmhand with his pitchfork and grain shovel is a thing of the past. Even a small-scale beef operation now needs automated feeding equipment. The conveyor-fed troughs are linked to oxygen-limiting silos that largely eliminate spoilage of their contents. They permit cutting and storing hay and other silage when it reaches a peak of nutritional content; open-air drying, which destroys food value, is reduced to a minimum.

Courtesy, A. O. Smith Harvestore Products, Inc.

Courtesy, The Goodyear Tire & Rubber Co.

Partial mechanization makes many hand operations in agricultural production easier and more efficient. These cascade lines of conveyor belts move almonds past workers who inspect, grade, and sort them. More acreage in California is devoted to almond groves than to oranges. The crop is worth more than $90 million annually to growers.

Courtesy, McIlhenny Co.

Harvesting remains the most labor-intensive aspect of agriculture. Lettuce, soft fruits, and many other easily bruised crops are still picked by hand. These field workers are gathering tabasco peppers in Louisiana. The ripe peppers are an ingredient in a variety of hot sauces; green peppers are sold as chilis.

UNIONS AND AGRICULTURE

AP/Wide World Photos

The position of agriculture as a multibillion-dollar industry was evidenced in the early 1970s when the giant Teamsters Union moved in to organize field workers and to crush the smaller United Farm Workers Union (UFWU) in the process. Many large growers broke contracts with the UFWU—a union formed by field workers themselves, not outsiders, and headed by Cesar Chavez—and hired Teamster labor instead. Growers were influenced by the favorable terms—virtual sweetheart deals in some cases—the Teamsters offered to speed their takeover, and by the fact that the Teamsters also effectively controlled the trucking that moved perishable crops to shippers and wholesalers. The UFWU fought back with strikes and boycotts. Here, workers picket the vineyards of a grower in 1973 who had just signed a Teamster Union contract.

UPI/Bettmann

The United Farm Workers Union had won contracts with California grape growers after an almost continuous series of strikes from 1965 to 1970. That struggle had broadened the meaning of the union's fight to La Causa—civil rights for Mexican-Americans. In 1970 a new struggle began against lettuce producers for similar recognition. Here, union leader Cesar Chavez waves to supporters as he leaves jail. He was imprisoned for two weeks for refusing to call off a lettuce boycott, but was released by order of the California Supreme Court.

UPI/Bettmann

Management and other white collar workers took to the fields to harvest lettuce during the UFWU strike. Such efforts were minimal, for many growers hired rival Teamster workers or brought in nonunion pickers—both illegal practices where the UFWU had a contract—in desperate attempts to harvest the crop before it spoiled in the fields.

SLIPPING THROUGH THE GOLDEN DOOR

AP/Wide World Photos

The pressure by poor people to get into the United States from countries to our south increased every year. America offered almost unbelievable abundance and opportunity compared to the situation of most. Especially in the Southwest, illegal immigration swelled to an uncontrollable tide as people entered from Mexico to satisfy the demand for cheap labor, especially for agricultural harvesting. Some came as "wetbacks," crossing the Rio Grande or other border rivers at night. Others were smuggled in by labor "contractors" using small trucks with concealed space like this, or packing forty or more people into larger trucks that tried to evade the insufficient border patrols of the U. S. Immigration Service.

An unexpected wave of thousands of Cubans entered the United States in May 1960 when Premier Fidel Castro suddenly announced a limited period in which political dissidents were free to leave. He managed to expel a number of criminals and mentally unbalanced individuals in the process. Hundreds were temporarily housed in improvised dormitories set up in the hangars of Eglin Air Force Base, Florida.

UPI/Bettmann

UPI/Bettmann

Haiti, the poorest country in the Western Hemisphere, generates a stream of thousands who attempt to enter the United States illegally each year. Some are smuggled in, others slip in undetected, and still others are intercepted by the Coast Guard. These are a few of the 135 refugees who crowded onto a forty-five-foot boat in April 1980 to make the crossing to Florida.

UPI/Bettmann

Resentment of immigrants increased greatly during the recession of the 1970s, when unemployment soared. Every additional person meant that much more competition for a job. This scene is at the Chicago City Hall in January 1975, where more than 2,000 people stood in line to apply for one of 987 jobs created with federal funds. Unemployment continued to be a major problem in the early 1980s because government used it as a means to cut inflation. Only in 1984 did Congress begin to seriously work on the problem of the impact of illegal immigration on the nation's economy.

4.

ENERGY
AND
ECOLOGY

America came to an abrupt confrontation with two major, related problems in the 1970s. One was that fuel and energy needs had grown unchecked: A seemingly limitless supply at bargain prices had encouraged reckless, wasteful consumption for decades. The other problem was destruction of the environment. Methods of obtaining fuels and generating energy for industrial and domestic purposes ruined millions of acres of land each year and raised water and air pollution to near-disastrous levels in some areas. Often the affected locations were hundreds of miles away from the source of pollution. Reaction to the realities of these problems was strong, but necessary adjustments were made only slowly and grudgingly. More often than not, strong government prodding was required. Solutions were elusive, and the efforts to find them seemed to slacken each time there was a slight easing of a problem.

The first rude awakening came in late 1973. A number of countries in the Middle East and South America formed a cartel dubbed OPEC—the Organization of Petroleum Exporting Countries. Their purpose was to regain control of the oil production facilities in their countries, which had been built and were operated by the giant refiners of the oil-consuming West, and also to raise the world price of oil to match the inflation-driven costs of other materials and products. OPEC's first move was to sharply reduce oil exports, which led to fuel-supply crises in Europe and America. De facto rationing created long lines at gas stations (*below*), where only a limited quantity could be purchased, and only on a day that was odd or even, corresponding to the last digit of the vehicle's license plate number.

AP/Wide World Photos

GASOLINE ALLEY

Courtesy, Buick Motor Div., General Motors Corp.

As a result of continued concern over fuel supply and consumption, American automobile manufacturers began to change the engineering design of their products. From major emphasis on large, luxurious cars like the 1973 Buick Electra (*above*), they turned to producing compact models such as the 1982 Chevrolet Cavalier (*below*). Reduced overall size and weight, and smaller engines—four rather than eight cylinders—were the major factors in delivering up to twice as much mileage per gallon. It took almost a decade for this change to occur in domestic manufacture, and it came only when American drivers began buying large numbers of small, fuel-efficient cars made in Europe and Japan, where they had been produced for thirty years.

Courtesy, Chevrolet Motor Division, General Motors Corp.

Photo by Robert Yarnall Richie, *courtesy*, Texaco

Gasoline stations changed, too. The full-service station (*above*) had evolved during the 1950s and 1960s. It occupied a large area, had attendant-operated pumps, and had one or more mechanics on duty for major or minor repairs and maintenance. By the 1980s, most stations were sleeker in design (*below*) and had reduced facilities in order to operate efficiently and profitably while coping with greatly increased operating and fuel costs. Gasoline was offered at self-service pump islands at ten to fifteen cents a gallon cheaper than at attended pumps, building were little more than an office and storeroom, and services were limited to oil and tire changing, and battery charging—or not even that. Even air pumps became coin operated, to recover the increased cost of electricity required to run the compressor.

Courtesy, Texaco

Courtesy, Alyeska Pipeline Service Co.

DOMESTIC RESOURCES

Although America produces most of its own oil, the impact of OPEC's sudden seizure of Middle East oil production, and of the more than triple increase in price that resulted, spurred efforts to locate and develop additional sources at home. The federal government quickly granted leases for offshore exploratory drilling in remote areas. Leases for drilling near more populous areas such as the coasts of New Jersey and California were far more controversial. The *Alaskan Star* (*opposite, above*) was the first rig to begin drilling in the Gulf of Alaska, in 1976. Discovery of large-scale oil reserves in the far north led to construction of an 800-mile pipeline (*opposite, below*) across Alaska. Every joint had to be welded, X-rayed, and pressure tested. Completed in 1977, the pipeline (*below*) can pump more than 1 million barrels a day from Prudhoe Bay on the Arctic Ocean coast to the ice-free port of Valdez, on the southern coast, where it is transferred to ocean-going tankers.

Courtesy, Alyeska Pipeline Service Co.

Between 1974 and 1982, the cost of oil and natural gas for home heating increased more than 400 percent. As a result, a vast new market developed in energy-saving products. New building construction had to meet higher requirements of heat conservation and fuel consumption. The federal government offered an income-tax credit for improving existing housing by adding insulation, storm windows, high-efficiency furnaces, solar heating units, and similar devices. Although the initial cost might be high, the tax credit and the savings in fuel costs would repay the investment in a few years. In the retrofit shown here, an exterior wall of a house has been covered with foil and new studs have been added to create spaces that will be filled with insulation before the outer sheathing and siding are put in place. The foil will act as a vapor barrier, blocking penetration of warm, moist air from the house interior into the insulation, where it would condense in cold weather, greatly reducing the insulation's efficiency.

Photo by Vernon M. Tryon

USING THE ATOM

One potential solution to dependence on oil is the use of nuclear fuels to produce the steam that drives the turbines in electrical power generating stations. The first such nuclear-powered plant in the United States began operation in 1961. Two decades later there were plants in fifty-one locations, producing three times as much electricity as nuclear plants in any other country. Expensive from the first, construction costs soared so high by 1982 that work on some partly finished facilities was stopped and plans for many other plants were abandoned. In addition, demands for electricity were running lower than the predictions of ten years before. The two major unsolved problems in nuclear energy production are safe disposal of waste material and protection against accidents. In March 1979, the Three Mile Island nuclear plant in Pennsylvania (*below*) was shut down after five years of operation, when extensive leakage of radioactive water and uncontrolled discharge of radioactive steam were discovered. Although no deaths or proximate injuries occurred, the long-term effects are unknown and the implications are frightening. It was the most serious accident in U. S. nuclear power history. The government responded with an extended investigation, and with far more stringent inspection, testing, and operating regulations.

Courtesy, Idaho State Historical Society

The United States National Reactor Testing Station is located on the Snake River plains near Arco, Idaho. Here, reactors—the units that produce a controlled nuclear chain reaction and use the energy to convert water to steam—are tested and evaluated for use in power stations, ships, submarines, and other applications.

Courtesy, Con Edison

The Indian Point nuclear power plant at Buchanan, New York, began operation in June 1973. After a leak of radioactive water, it was shut down in March 1982.

UPI/Bettmann

Convinced that government regulations were too permissive and that inspection and control were lax, protest groups opposed the construction or operation of nuclear plants in a number of locations. Here, State Police load demonstrators onto buses in 1977, clearing the site of a proposed plant at Seabrook, New Hampshire.

SPILLS AND POISONS

Pollution of coastal waters by oil from damaged tankers, drilling or
loading accidents, and rigs destroyed by storms has become a repeated
problem in the past twenty years. The flotation barrier towed by two
ships here is one way of containing oil spills in relatively calm waters.
This test, using nonpolluting soybean oil, was photographed by ob-
servers aboard the airship for study and evaluation.

Courtesy, The Goodyear Tire & Rubber Co.

Courtesy, U. S. Dept. of Agriculture, Soil Conservation Service

Unregulated waste disposal into waterways, sneak dumping, or wash-out and leaching from the surrounding earth can cause problems like this detergent-filled stream in Alabama. Fish and plants are killed, and the water is made unfit for human use.

Few sources of contaminated water are clearly marked like this one. And what good is this sign to someone a short way downstream, or someone whose well receives seepage from this source? Similar problems on a much larger scale began to receive long-needed attention in the 1970s from the Environmental Protection Agency. Then, in the 1980s, the administration of Ronald Reagan reduced federal participation in pollution control on the grounds of not interfering with the responsibilities of state and local governments, and not restricting needed industrial growth.

The effects of pollution are cumulative. Pollutants build up to very high toxicities in the slow-current eddies along the banks and around the wharves of even fast-moving rivers. The fish and plant life that prefer these locations are killed; as they decay they add further pollution. Over a period of time, vast areas can be destroyed, as was the case with the spawning grounds for striped bass in the Hudson and Chesapeake rivers. Only vigorous enforcement of antipollution regulations and long-term, massive clean-up efforts made headway against the conditions in these waters.

Antipollution, pro-conservation advocates staged Earth Day celebrations across the country each Spring in the early 1970s. Their purpose was to emphasize the need for concern about ecology—the interaction of living organisms with one another and with their environment, and the delicate balance that maintains the health and character of a natural area. A second purpose was to call attention to the ways in which humans upset that balance and destroyed the ecology. These students are paddling homemade craft on Earth Day 1970 to protest the polluted condition of the Milwaukee River.

UPI/Bettmann

Courtesy, U. S. Dept. of Agriculture, Soil Conservation Service

Increased consumption and increased pollution have made the problem of getting safe water a serious concern in many areas. Here, pipe is being delivered to build a conduit that will bypass this pond and channel snow-melt run-off to the Bede Reservoir in Colorado.

Pollution that goes into the air may travel hundreds of miles before people breathe it in, or before it settles to earth to become part of what they eat and drink. Some pollutants wash out of the air as acid rain, which destroys plant life and poisons lakes. Among the major culprits are factories like this that first shatter the surrounding area to get raw materials, then spew waste into the air as they process the materials.

Courtesy, National Archives. Photo by Billy Davis, *Louisville Courier-Journal*

Courtesy, American Iron and Steel Institute

Industry does not have to pollute to operate successfully. Pollution control equipment on this giant furnace collects and recycles over 99 percent of the dust generated in the steelmaking process.

Courtesy, American Automobile Association

Vehicles are also a major source of air pollution, especially in the commuting crushes that afflict almost every city twice a day. (*Above*) Express lanes for multiple-passenger vehicles such as buses relieve both transportation and pollution problems simultaneously. (*Below*) Electrically powered streetcars, once a feature of every medium- and large-size American city, disappeared in the era of cheap gasoline and diesel fuel and metropolitan expansion following World War II. Now they are reappearing in a few places—such as San Diego, shown here—because they are economically competitive again and because they reduce the air pollution and curb-lane congestion created by buses.

Courtesy, San Diego Metropolitan Transit Development Board

Courtesy, Chicago Transit Authority

Central-city mass transit is a nightmare in many cities, but some areas have been able to maintain or create efficient transportation to and from outlying areas. (*Above*) A station on the suburban service of the Chicago Transit Authority. (*Below*) Inside a car on BART—the Bay Area Rapid Transit system—in San Francisco. The first entirely new system built in the United States since World War II, it features automatic operation.

Courtesy, San Francisco Bay Area Rapid Transit District

UNDER THE GROUND

Four cities—London, Boston, Paris, and Berlin—had subways before New York City's was opened in 1904, but no city comes close to its two hundred miles of lines. No system matches it for deterioration and maintenance problems, either. While some parts of the New York system have modern, air-conditioned cars in excellent condition, the equipment that serves the most depressed areas of the city suffers from vandalism, graffiti (*below*), and lack of attention. The problem is as much one of social attitudes of the passengers as it is one of labor and management problems of the New York Transit Authority. Some aspects of the subway-riding experience were sensationalized in "Lexington Avenue Local" (*opposite*), part of a complex "Ruckus Manhattan" sculpture created in 1965 by artist Red Grooms and his students.

Courtesy, National Archives

Creative Time, Inc.

FLIGHTS OF FANCY

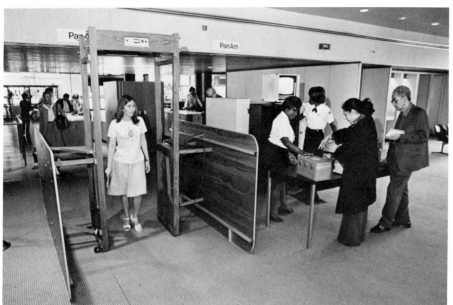

Courtesy, Pan American World Airways

Air travel, more extensive than ever, took on a permanent air of security consciousness in the 1970s (*above*). Repeated highjacking of planes by revolutionaries and dissidents made X-ray examination of all carry-on items standard procedure at airports. In addition, passengers had to pass through metal detectors. Too many keys or bracelets meant putting the offending items in a basket and walking through again, until the alarm remained silent.

(*Below*) The air was also more crowded with communications than ever before. Land lines and point-to-point microwave relays gave way to ground–space–ground satellite relays that could cover half a continent or more with multiple channels for television, radio, telephone, and computer communications. On the individual level, in 1984 passenger telephone calls from airliners in flight were introduced. It seemed almost impossible to be out of touch.

Courtesy, AT&T Corporate Archive

Photo by McDonnell Douglas

A steady increase in intercontinental air traffic was accommodated by the new DC-10 (*above*) and similar aircraft in the 1970s, capable of carrying up to 345 passengers at reasonable operating costs. The glamor plane of the decade, the supersonic Concorde (*below*), was technologically advanced and much faster than other passenger airliners. However, its multibillion-dollar development costs, high operating costs, and limited passenger capacity caused the major airlines to decide against buying it as standard equipment. The governments of Britain and France, which had developed the plane jointly, had to subsidize its continued operation. Logistics rather than equipment were the major American aviation problems in the early 1980s. The air traffic controllers went on strike in a labor dispute with the government, an illegal action. They were all dismissed by President Reagan and several thousand new controllers were trained in a short period of time. In 1984, the Federal Aviation Commission threatened new regulations to break the logjam of too many scheduled arrivals and departures at peak airports in all major locations. The airlines quickly moved to change schedules voluntarily rather than accept increased government control.

Courtesy, Air France

5.

BUILDING
AMERICA

Urban renewal, which had become a major concern during the previous decade, expanded in the 1970s. Large-scale, architecturally grandiose projects were favored because they readily won federal funding assistance and conferred prestige on the public officials, designers, and builders concerned. Commercial-use buildings concentrated on simple design and increasing height to get the maximum return for a given investment; public-use structures such as auditoriums generally showed greater experimentation in outward appearance. Attention to residential housing needs turned from vast slum-clearance projects to a slowly developing concern with preserving and restoring the existing architectural stock. "Landmark" designation brought public assistance to some buildings of potential historic interest. Private buyers found it economically worthwhile to renovate hundreds of thousands of solidly built late-nineteenth-century row houses in the nation's older cities. Conversion of old downtown-area office and manufacturing buildings into high-priced cooperative and condominium living units and specialty shops accelerated late in the decade. The displacement of low-income families and small industries was largely ignored until the 1980s, when long-standing government promises of remedy slowly began to be acted upon. The period also saw a great migration of population to the "sun belt" states of the south and southwest, increased movement of minorities into the suburbs immediately adjacent to large cities, and some return of affluent, late-middle-aged couples from the suburbs to newly furbished housing in the cities. However, inflation and economic uncertainty pushed the American dream of owning a home beyond the reach of most young married couples by the early 1980s.

PAST AND FUTURE

Courtesy, Missouri Division of Tourism

Riverfront cities in America developed outward from the central wharves and landings. These locations were the focal points for urban renewal. (*Above*) St. Louis, Missouri, became the entry city to the heartland of America well before the Civil War, when paddle-wheel steamers were the major mode of transporation on the Mississippi River. This gateway role is symbolized by the 630-foot stainless-steel Jefferson National Expansion Memorial arch, designed by Eero Saarinen and erected in 1963 when rebuilding of the center city began. (*Below*) Renaissance Center, on the Detroit riverfront, was a bold attempt to rejuvenate a deteriorated downtown area. Large tracts were cleared and the first results were positive, but in the early 1980s the center faced bankruptcy in the economically devastated Motor City.

Courtesy, U. S. Department of Housing and Urban Development

Courtesy, Houston Chamber of Commerce

Much center-city renewal has consisted of commercial-use skyscrapers.
A straight-shaft design offers maximum occupancy—and thus rental
income—for the least expense in land, foundation, structure, and
facilities. As a result, the skyline of what were once low-profile cities
has changed dramatically. In less than a decade, Houston, Texas
(*above*), had become a skyscraper city by 1971. It continues to be one
of the fastest-growing cities in the country. In Portland, Oregon (*below*),
a skyscraper banking center dominates high-rise growth. Mount Hood
is seen in the distance, across the Willamette River.

Courtesy, State of Oregon

THE TALLEST

High-rise design has been a major twentieth-century opportunity for architectural achievement. The Empire State and Chrysler buildings, erected in New York City in the late 1930s, were the world's tallest (1,250 and 1,046 feet, respectively) for almost four decades. In the 1970s an unacknowledged competition in tall-structure architecture developed. By 1984 there were more than fifty-five buildings 700 feet or taller in the United States, more than in all the rest of the world.

Chicago boasts the world's tallest building, the Sears Tower. Designed by Bruce John Graham with Skidmore, Owings, and Merrill, and completed in 1974, its 110 stories rise to a height of 1,454 feet.

Courtesy, Sears, Roebuck and Co.

Courtesy, The Port Authority of New York and New Jersey

The dramatic twin towers and surrounding plaza buildings of the World Trade Center sparked development of a new business and residential complex, Battery Park City, at the southern end of Manhattan. The 110-story, 1,350-foot towers, designed by Minoru Yamasaki and Emery Roth, were ready for occupancy in 1970.

Gorchev & Gorchev Photography

The John Hancock Tower in Boston, designed by I. M. Pei, is one of America's most striking glass-wall buildings. It rises 790 feet between the Italian Renaissance public library and the Romanesque Holy Trinity Church of Henry Hobson Richardson.

Courtesy, Westin Hotels and John Portman & Associates

(*Above*) The cylindrical Peachtree Plaza Hotel in Atlanta, Georgia, designed by John Portman, is the world's tallest hotel (722 feet). Elevators in the external shaft along one side can reach the top in eighty seconds. (*Below*) A restaurant at the top of the hotel rotates about once an hour, providing a panorama of the Queen City of the South.

Courtesy, Westin Hotels and John Portman & Associates

EXPRESSIVE DESIGN

Public funding of memorial buildings and facilities for cultural activities has traditionally freed architects from economic constraints on design. In some cases harmony with the surroundings has been the major design criterion, in other cases, the prestige of unique appearance. In the 1970s, most such structures presented bold shapes or facades but relied on conventional structural methods and interior design.

An exterior of quiet modern classicism complements the restrained elegance of the interior of the John F. Kennedy Center for the Performing Arts, on the Potomac River. (For a view of the interior, see page 195.) Although large enough to house a concert hall, opera house, and film and drama theaters, its horizontal proportions harmonize with the low-profile character of public buildings throughout Washington, D. C.

Courtesy, Washington, D.C., Convention and Visitors Association

Courtesy, Texas State Department of Highways—Travel and Information Division

The fortresslike design of the Alley Theatre in the Houston, Texas, Civic Center houses two separate theaters. It was completed in 1968.

Ezra Stoller © ESTO Photographics, Inc.

Modernism in architecture originated at the German Bauhaus in the 1920s. The style is perpetuated in the Bronx Developmental Center, designed by Richard Meier and built in New York City in the early 1970s. (For a residential design by the same architect, see page 126).

Courtesy, Dallas Chamber of Commerce

The enormous outer walls of the John Fitzgerald Kennedy Memorial in Dallas, Texas, create a massive hollow cube. At its center is a block of black granite engraved with the name of the president who was assassinated here in 1963. It was designed by Philip Johnson, considered by many to be the premier American architect of the mid-twentieth century.

Courtesy, U. S. Department of Housing and Urban Development

A national desire to save America's architectural heritage matured in the 1970s. The preservation and restoration of historic buildings such as these in Washington, D. C., was aided by federal and local landmark legislation to protect whole neighborhoods as well as individual sites.

Courtesy, Jacob K. Javits Convention Center of New York

One example of landmark preservation of an entire area is the South Street Seaport Museum in lower Manhattan. The buildings seen here have since been restored to their condition in the early nineteenth century, when they were a bustling center of seafaring activity. Additional old sailing vessels have been restored as permanent exhibits at the water side.

Attracting shoppers as well as office workers downtown became essential to prevent the migration of retail businesses to suburban plazas. One solution was the mall—an area closed to vehicles, with amenities that made it both easy and pleasant for pedestrians to move from store to store, and then to adjacent parking areas and public transportation.

In the old manufacturing town of Troy, New York, the glass facade of the Uncle Sam Mall encloses shops and restaurants, and wide corridors that customers prefer to the ample exterior walkways in the cold months and bad weather.

Courtesy, U. S. Department of Housing and Urban Development

(*Above*) Shopping is easy along the meandering, tree-lined Nicollet Mall in downtown Minneapolis. The broad sidewalks are heated to eliminate snow, ice, and cold feet in the winter.

(*Below*) Baltimore replaced much of its old Victorian waterfront shop world with Harbor Palace, an elegant new city center with facilities for both commercial and leisure activities.

Courtesy, U. S. Department of Housing and Urban Development

Courtesy, New York State Office of General Services. Photo by Don Doremus

The Empire State Plaza in Albany, capital of New York State, is an example of the massive office-complex mall as an element of urban renewal. In this 1975 photograph, the South Mall is still under construction.

HOUSING AMERICA

Residents of deteriorated neighborhoods grew increasingly resentful when urban renewal concentrated on historic and business areas, leaving them with nothing but broken promises and devastated conditions year after year. A major part of the problem was that low-income families could not afford rents that would repay the costs of rehabilitation. This 1980 scene is in the South Bronx section of New York City.

Courtesy, U. S. Department of Housing and Urban Development

Courtesy, Vermont Travel Division

The New England countryside and villages such as East Corinth, Vermont, have remained virtually unchanged for many generations. While such scenes perpetuate a classic, often idealized image of American life, in fact less than 30 percent of the nation's population lives in small towns and rural areas.

Photo © Michael Heron 1981/Woodfin Camp & Associates

Owning a home is the hope of the great majority of Americans. In the 1960s and 1970s the house of choice was a ranch-style—meaning one-story—design, located in the suburbs. This was often modified with a two-story section to accommodate a larger family on a standard-size lot. Both styles are seen *above* in a suburban area near Raleigh, North Carolina. A larger lot, with full landscaping and greater seclusion from neighbors—like the Asheville, North Carolina, home *below*—added considerably to the cost.

Courtesy, Asheville Area Chamber of Commerce

REHAB—OR PREFAB?

Home ownership had become an impossible dream for many young families by the early 1980s. Mortgage interest rates were in the over 15 percent range, and the price of a newly constructed one-family house went above $100,000. These were historic highs, unaffordable by most. Builders tried to keep costs down by reducing overall size, eliminating recreation rooms and fully finished basements, offering carports in place of garages, and by increasing the use of prefabricated units (see the next two pages). An alternative was to rehabilitate an existing house, a growing trend that helped save decaying neighborhoods in many cities. Generally, brick and stone houses built from the 1870s to about 1915 were the best candidates for rehabilitation. Much wood-frame construction of the 1920s through the 1940s, like the houses *below*, was physically or economically beyond saving. Although such structures provided needed housing for the poor, their days were numbered. Each year the need for replacement housing as well as new construction grew faster than the supply. This, and constantly rising prices for labor and materials, also pushed home prices higher.

Courtesy, U. S. Department of Housing and Urban Development

Courtesy, Automated Building Components, Inc.; New York Public Library Picture Collection

Prefabrication cuts labor costs significantly. Houses are constructed at the factory in two or three sections, complete with electrical wiring and plumbing. These are trucked to the site and hoisted into place. On-site exterior and interior finishing time is reduced to less than half that of conventional construction methods.

Some houses are composed of several prefabricated modules. The number and assembly configuration of the modules can be varied to create houses of different sizes and designs from a few standard units. The modular approach has been tried in some cities, placing semifinished apartment units into the structural frame of a large building that has been gutted. Although a significant amount of on-site work is required to interconnect all units and finish the building, the cost is much lower than constructing a new apartment complex.

Courtesy, U. S. Department of Housing and Urban Development

Courtesy, U. S. Department of Housing and Urban Development

These assembled Levitt factory-built houses in King County, Washington, show that prefabrication can offer varied and interesting exterior design.

THE INSIDE STORY

This display living room shows an eclectic taste that was very popular in the 1970s. Finished wood cabinets contrast with the random-filled stone and rough post-and-beam mantel of the through-fireplace wall. Stuffed barrel chairs are combined with a cylindrical end table, contemporary square-corner upholstered pieces, and tables derived from a classic Chinese design.

Courtesy, Drexel Heritage Furnishings, Inc.

Courtesy, Magic Chef, Inc.

A spacious, fully equipped modern kitchen is one of the first features most middle-class American families look for in choosing a home.

LIVING WITH NATURE

These two Florida houses, designed by William Morgan, combine very modern style and a physical integration with the environment. The hilltop house *below* offers a patio with ample sun and shade areas and an upper deck for sunning. The large upper and lower windows provide a spacious view and admit a great deal of light, but are set well back to avoid the direct rays of the sun. Sunk into the natural slope of the hill, the structure is insulated year round by the surrounding earth.

Photo by Creative Photographic Services, *courtesy*, William Morgan Architects

Courtesy, William Morgan Architects

(*Above*) This unusual beach house takes its outer form from the hillocks and dunes of its surroundings. The sod outer layer helps keep the covering earth in place. The eyelike "windows" are in front of small patios. Their shape seems far more appropriate to the site than rectangular openings would.

(*Below*) The view from within is like looking from inside some giant creature, perhaps Jonah's whale.

Photo by Alexander Georges, *courtesy*, William Morgan Architects

Ezra Stoller © ESTO Photographics, Inc.

Innovations in residential architecture were both more unusual and more expensive than ever in the 1970s. The choice of a dramatic but remote private location could easily double the total cost of a project. The Douglas House (*above left*), set among the dark spruce of Harbor Springs, Michigan, was designed by Richard Meier, who is noted for the technological modernism of his style (see page 110). The home of architect Charles Deaton (*below left*) features a folded-circle design that looks startlingly as if a UFO had landed in the Colorado mountains.

Courtesy, Charles Deaton, Architect

6.

SOCIAL
CONSCIOUSNESS

The civil rights struggles of the 1960s were the beginning of major changes in American society. The extent of these changes became clearer in the 1970s as legislation passed in the Kennedy and Johnson administrations had time to take effect. Several minority groups in addition to blacks began to demand equality of treatment. They included American Indians, the handicapped, and homosexuals and lesbians. By far the largest group—numerically a majority, but treated as a minority socially, politically, and legally—was women. The National Organization for Women—NOW—was founded in 1966 to focus attention on women's problems. After an initial period of consciousness-raising to emphasize the common plight of women at all levels, NOW turned to political action and demanded addition of an equal rights amendment (ERA) to the United States Constitution. The ERA was only twenty-four words long: "Equality of rights under the law shall not be denied or abridged by the United States or by any state on account of sex." Hawaii was the first state to ratify the amendment, two hours after its passage by Congress in 1972; within a year, thirty states had voted ratification. But few more followed suit; some reactionary women even organized opposition. In June 1982, after a three-year and three-month extension of the approval period, the ERA died, just three states short of the thirty-eight ratifications required for its adoption.

In the meantime, political activity by women had increased enormously. The National Women's Political Caucus demanded—unsuccessfully, but not without some effect—that half the delegates to the 1972 presidential nominating conventions be women, a proportion that would nearly match their position in the total population. Leaders of the caucus (*below*) were New York Congresswoman Bella Abzug (standing), and (seated, left to right) Gloria Steinem, a founder of *Ms* magazine; New York Congresswoman Shirley Chisholm; and Betty Friedan, founder of NOW.

AP/Wide World Photos

"MY BODY, MY CHOICE"

Two extremely personal individual rights became the focus of major action in the 1970s: pregnancy and sexual preference. One aspect of the pregnancy question was whether schools and government agencies should provide birth-control information. Far more important, and emotional, was the issue of abortion. Those in favor of legalized abortions argued that a woman's body was her own, that only she had the right to decide whether to terminate a pregnancy or give birth, and that she was entitled to medical assistance whatever her decision. Those opposed argued that the fetus was an individual with civil rights, including the right to life; thus, abortion was murder, not to be condoned by law nor supported by state or federal medical aid programs. Others were opposed on moral or religious grounds, and some would even deny abortion in cases of pregnancy by rape or incest. Initial confrontations, like the one *below* outside the New Jersey Legislature in the early 1970s, were over the issue of government assistance. Increasing political conservatism and militant religious fundamentalism later in the decade resulted in arson and bomb attacks on clinics offering abortions in some locations, and in scathing personal attacks on individuals. The issue became part of the 1984 presidential campaign, when the Democratic vice-presidential candidate was both a woman and a Catholic, Geraldine Ferraro. She opposed abortion on moral and religious grounds, but supported the right of each woman to decide for herself.

AP/Wide World Photos

Adopting the euphemism "gay" to distinguish themselves from the heterosexual majority, homosexuals and lesbians joined forces to demonstrate publicly for equal rights. In rallies and parades—*above*, Greenwich Village, New York, June 1974—they demanded an end to discrimination in housing, employment, laws, and police attention. Choice of a sexual partner was a private matter that should not be the cause of public reprisal, however subtle, they argued. As the Gay Liberation movement grew, it found the strength to demonstrate against the opposition, such as appearances of singer Anita Bryant with a fundamentalist crusade (*below*) in Norfolk, Virginia.

WOMEN'S CAREERS

AP/Wide World Photos

Women began to demand an end to job discrimination and a beginning of equal pay for work of equal difficulty or responsibility as that of men. The airline stewardesses (*above*) are demonstrating for their right to maternity leaves without losing their jobs. A related issue was the right not to be fired at an early age, presumably because they had grown less attractive than when hired, even though far more experienced. As discrimination broke down, men were also hired for this job, which was given the sexually neutral title of Flight Attendant.

Barbara Walters, shown at *right* interviewing author Truman Capote in 1967, was earning more than $400,000 a year by the mid-1970s, one of the highest salaries ever paid a woman other than a movie star. Even so, it was less than the salaries of several male television journalists of comparable position and achievement. In more mundane jobs, women could seldom rise to the same level as men, and almost never at equal pay.

UPI/Bettmann

Courtesy, U. S. Army News Features

The number of women in the United States Army doubled in a decade, to almost 76,000 in 1982. The number of women in the Air Force, Navy, and Marines totaled 112,000 in the same year. The Women's Army Corps (WAC) specialists *above* are preparing for an inspection at a noncommissioned officers training school. The WAC was disestablished in 1978 and women soldiers were integrated with the rest of the Army. The service academies began accepting women for officer training in 1973. The West Point cadets *below* are in a makeup class, one of the very few courses that male cadets do not also attend.

Courtesy, U. S. Army

In almost every field, women now were accepted for full-fledged professional training where once they had been limited to becoming assistants. These veterinary science students at Kansas State University are preparing a lamb for X-ray examination.

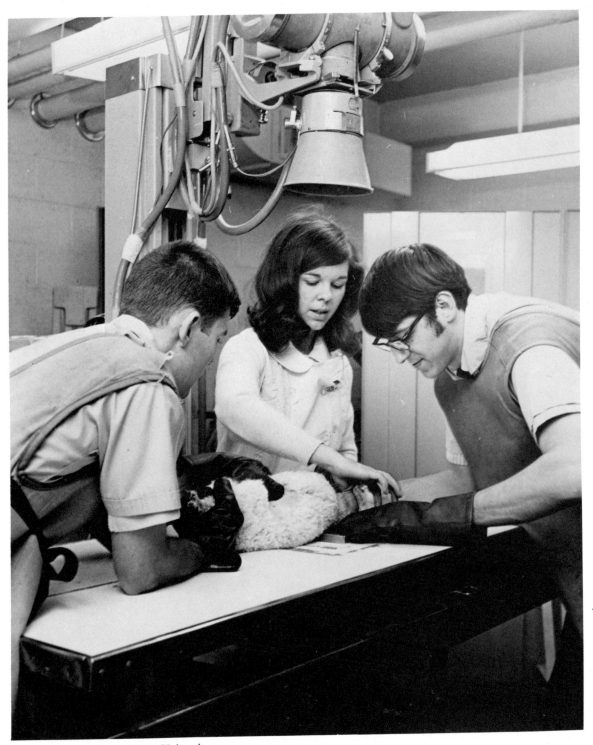

Courtesy, Kansas State University

Courtesy, AT&T Corporate Archive

Although World War II had brought great numbers of women into heavy-industry factories, their participation in blue-collar "male" jobs dropped to almost nothing in the next twenty-five years. Then, in the 1970s, job sex-discrimination began to give way in the face of legal challenges and changing social attitudes. Women became construction workers, electricians and plumbers, long-haul truck drivers, and many other kinds of "heavy job" laborers. Their number was not large at first, and they met a good deal of resistance and resentment, especially as unemployment climbed in the last half of the decade. But an irreversible trend was established. This woman landed a job as a telephone installer-repairperson with Southern Bell in Florida in the early 1970s.

NATIVE AMERICANS

Deprived of land and rights almost from the first arrival of white settlers, the Indians of America had been reduced to a small, poor, and exhausted minority. Civil rights advances in the 1960s and 1970s encouraged them to seek repayment for the fraudulent land seizures, abrogated treaties, and unconstitutional government actions of the last two hundred years. There were both victories and defeats, and internal disputes over tribal leadership and strategy. Court procedure was long, slow, and frustrating; in the face of immediate needs, some turned to direct action (see facing page). The Alaskan Eskimos won return of certain lands and restoration of exclusive hunting and fishing rights in some areas after a long legal battle. Those shown *below* are hauling a walrus onto the ice.

UPI/Bettmann

UPI/Bettmann

Outraged by generations of shabby treatment and neglect, militant American Indians seized the Bureau of Indian Affairs in Washington, D. C. (*left*) in November 1972. The protest ended peacefully, but, in February 1973, what has been called the last Indian battle broke out in Wounded Knee, South Dakota. A militant group seized buildings on the Oglala Sioux reservation (*below*) and demanded an investigation of alleged mismanagement and deceit by the Bureau of Indian Affairs. Two persons were killed before the protest was settled in May.

UPI/Bettmann

A NEW MILITANCY

Both those who would expand and those who would repress freedom
and civil rights formed militant action groups. In 1966, Huey P. Newton
and Bobby Seale founded the Black Panthers, a revolutionary action
party, in Oakland, California. They believed blacks had to arm themselves and engage in violence in order to win liberation in modern
America. After several battles with police in major cities and a number of deaths, a split in the movement developed in 1972. Newton and
Seale renounced violence, while Eldridge Cleaver took control of the
violent-action wing of the party, operating from exile in Algeria. *Below*,
George Murray, a prominent member of the Black Panthers, addresses
an Oakland rally in 1968, surrounded by guards in leather jackets and
berets, the party uniform. An upraised clenched fist, one of the party's
emblems, symbolized black power.

Photo © by Stephen Shames, Magnum Photos, Inc.

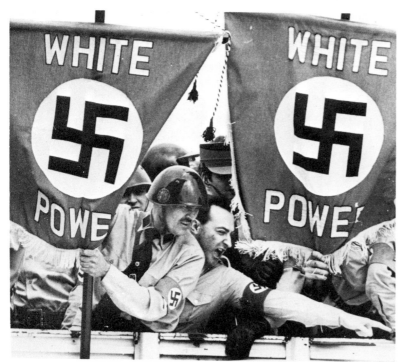

UPI/Bettmann

The evil of anti-Semitism and white supremacy reemerged in the form of the newly militant National Socialist (American Nazi) Party. *Above*, party director Frank Collins yells at anti-Nazi demonstrators along a parade route in south St. Louis, in March 1978. An April parade in Skokie, Illinois, the cause of much preliminary legal action, was canceled when the tiny but noisy party realized they could not march without being attacked. In New York, Rabbi Meir Kahane formed the Jewish Defense League to take violent reprisals against acts by anti-Jewish organizations and governments. *Below*, members of the JDL participate in a 1981 Salute to Israel parade up Fifth Avenue.

UPI/Bettmann

THE RIGHT TO LEARN EQUALLY

Federal legislation and court decisions had ended college-level discrimination in the 1960s. During the 1970s, federal courts ordered a redistribution of the secondary school population in many cities to achieve racial balance in the classroom. This was usually accomplished by transporting minority students to all-white schools and white students to minority-area schools. Some parents objected for thinly concealed reasons of racial prejudice, others because of the burden on children of having to ride up to an hour and a half each way on a school bus. One reaction among opponents was to boycott the schools. The scene here is a Memphis, Tennessee, classroom during a two-day boycott in April 1972, when some 50,000 students were kept home to protest court-ordered busing that was not to begin until September.

UPI/Bettmann

UPI/Bettmann

Cities varied in their acceptance of busing. After a period of turmoil, Louisville, Kentucky, adjusted to busing (*above*), and in 1976 this mode of integration was peacefully accepted. In contrast, school buses from minority areas required police guards against violence for several years as they passed through white working-class sections of Boston and some other northern cities. In some areas, white parents withdrew their children rather than have them bused to inner-city schools. The children *below* are attending school at home in a Los Angeles residential area. Their tutors are two teachers hired by neighborhood parents.

AP/Wide World Photos

THE RIGHT TO VOTE

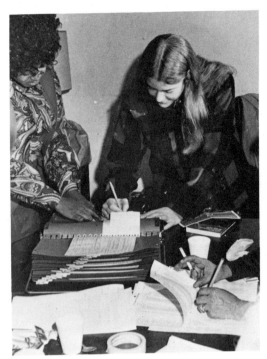

AP/Wide World Photos

The twenty-sixth amendment to the Constitution lowered the federal voting age to eighteen. It was ratified in June 1971, making some 11½ million young Americans eligible to vote in the election the next year (*above*) that returned Richard Nixon to office for a second term as president. Women had been given the vote with ratification of the nineteenth amendment in 1920. That battle had been fought for fifty years by Susan B. Anthony (*below, right*), who died fourteen years before the final victory. In her honor, the government issued a new silver dollar (*below, left*) in 1979. It was not a success, primarily because it was almost the same size as the U.S. quarter and easily confused with it.

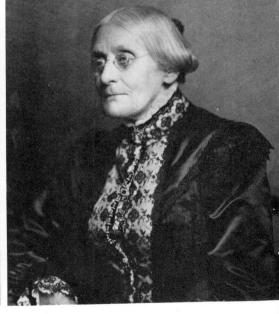

Courtesy, Library of Congress

THE RIGHTS OF THE HANDICAPPED

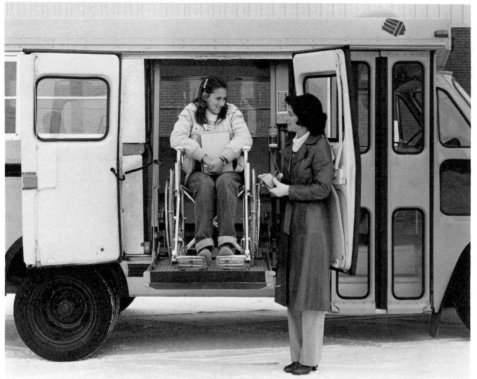

Courtesy, Wayne Corporation

The decade saw significant progress in providing equal access to public facilities for the physically handicapped. Federal regulations and matching state laws required provision for the handicapped in return for funding assistance. Improved vehicles (*above*) came into service for school transportation, and standard buses were modified to accept wheelchairs. Public buildings were equipped with telephones (*below*), toilets, entrance ramps, and other features that accommodated wheelchairs or otherwise met special physical requirements.

Courtesy, San Francisco Bay Area Rapid Transit (BART)

THE RIGHT TO LIFE-STYLE

Photo © Jim Anderson 1978/Woodfin Camp & Associates

Two segments of the population grew in size and influence in the 1970s. Teenagers (*above*) gained more social independence and economic power than ever before. Their life-style was unconventional and "hippie" early in the decade, but by 1980 a far more conservative manner and appearance had become the norm. The over-fifty-five age group (*right*) also became larger, more active, and more politically influential. The image of a senior citizen as incompetent and dependent crumbled rapidly as the nation began to appreciate the rewarding aspects of later life.

Courtesy, Washington State Travel Photo

7.

DAILY
LIFE

The major social changes in American life discussed in earlier chapters —domestic turmoil over war and politics, urban renewal, civil rights activism, ecological concerns, and similar matters—were accompanied by a continuous series of small changes in everyday life. Seldom a matter of headlines, these changes had a cumulative effect that produced significant differences between the late 1960s and the late 1970s. Perhaps the greatest change was in the cost of living. As retail sales of consumer goods increased, prices increased at a greater rate, sparked in part by rising energy and labor costs for manufacturers and producers. The resulting "double-digit" (i.e., above 10 percent) inflation rate also affected the financial markets, and the prime interest rate reached a record high of 21 percent. In the early 1980s, economic measures taken by President Ronald Reagan cut these rates by one-third to one-half, but only by creating a surge in unemployment and an economic recession that many felt came dangerously close to a full-fledged depression. From houses to shoelaces, prices were a matter of concern to everyone. The shopper *below* is hesitating over the purchase of coffee, which had reached a "ridiculous" price level in 1977, as noted on the sign from the store president. Consumer and retailer boycotts of expensive products had little effect on producers and wholesalers, however.

UPI/Bettmann

THE CONSUMER

Courtesy, The Grand Union Company

Americans' awareness of food and its preparation developed selectivity and sophistication in the 1970s. Cooking paid more attention to natural flavors and avoided fats, frying, and cream sauces. Those who could meet rising prices sought out unusual and fashionable items. Specialty food shops and restaurants appeared almost everywhere and supermarkets installed "gourmet" sections (*above*) to meet the demand. Other Americans turned to raising their own food for reasons of economy and concern for nutrition. The goat milking (*below*) is taking place on a rural commune, where several families have combined to live in near self-sufficiency. A popular mode of life for some independent young people that originated in the 1960s, the commune movement dwindled significantly after about 1975.

Camera Five

Courtesy, Hawaii Visitors Bureau

The suburban shopping mall reached new levels of size and elegance. A mall brings both specialty and mass-market stores together in an arrangement that offers customers wide choice, convenience, and protection from the weather. Usually the mall is the center of a many-acre shopping plaza that includes department stores, supermarkets, furniture stores and appliance dealers, movie theaters, a variety of restaurants, and parking for hundreds or even thousands of cars. The photograph *above* shows the mall of the Ala Moana Center in Hawaii.

SHARED CULTURES

America's growth depended on the skills and talents brought here by immigrants from all over the world. In 1961, President John F. Kennedy established the Peace Corps to help take skills to people in underdeveloped countries. American volunteers worked abroad to teach language, agriculture, construction, improved hand skills, and many other subjects in countries with little or no industrial development and high rates of illiteracy. In the 1970 photo *below*, a volunteer occupational therapist is demonstrating basketry techniques in Nairobi, Kenya. By this time the Corps had more than eleven thousand volunteers and trainees in sixty countries. In 1971 it was combined with VISTA (Volunteers in Service to America, a kind of domestic Peace Corps for American neighborhoods) and several other federal volunteer aid programs in a State Department agency called Action. A decade later, budget cutbacks had reduced these programs to virtual skeletons.

Courtesy, United States Peace Corps/Action

AP/Wide World Photos

The familiar term "melting pot" suggests that the ethnic diversity of America becomes a great homogeneous blend. That is true in some aspects of life, but many groups keep their cultural heritage alive with great pride, especially on ceremonial occasions. *Above*, in New York's Chinatown and similar sections in other cities, firecrackers and dragons always welcome in the Chinese New Year. *Below*, sword dancing, caber tossing, and bagpipe music are some of the many traditional features of the annual Gathering of Scots and Highland Games in Austin, Texas.

Courtesy, Texas State Department of Highways—Travel and Information Division

STUDENT LIFE-STYLES

Campus life had been a turmoil of protest, demonstrations, and sit-ins in the 1960s. These rapidly disappeared by the mid-1970s, and along with them hippie and unconventional dress, grooming, and behavior. College students became more concerned with academic achievement and finding a job upon graduation. These and other developments prefigured the outright student conservatism of the 1980s. This scene is at Vassar, a women's college in Poughkeepsie, New York, which had become coeducational in 1969. Economic and social concerns caused many other all-male and all-female institutions to follow suit in the succeeding decade.

Courtesy, Vassar College

While dress and behavior returned to middle-class conventionality, male–female interaction on campus achieved a new degree of relaxed freedom. The two students *above* attend the University of Southern California. Many schools established coed dormitories that—despite the predictions of many self-appointed moralists—did not turn into dens of sexual activity. On campus and off (*below*), young women exhibited a new attitude toward fashion. Miniskirts coexisted with midis, and with jeans, long skirts, and many other styles. Whatever felt right was now acceptable; there was less concern than ever before about what might be "correct."

Women's Wear Daily/Fairchild

Women's Wear Daily

FASHION

Although the great majority of American women abandoned a slavish obedience to annual changes in fashion, they did not give up a sharp eye for what they considered a smart appearance. Great change is evident in comparing the tightly tailored minicoat and patterned stockings of 1968 (*below*) with the fuller, more flowing styles of the early 1980s (*opposite page*). Changes in hair styles and makeup are equally evident. Young black women stopped trying to do their hair like that of Caucasians and discovered the natural beauty of the Afro style (*below*). This was soon joined by an adaptation of a style traditional to many African tribes: parallel rows braided tightly to the skull, known as "corn-rows."

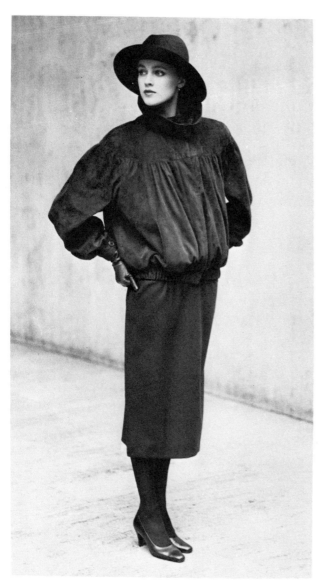

Women's Wear Daily/Fairchild

ART, ANCIENT AND MODERN

Museums and art galleries repeatedly attracted record-breaking numbers of visitors throughout the decade. Major museums around the world exchanged "blockbuster" exhibits with sister institutions. One of the most successful was "Treasures of Tutankhamun" (*above*), which drew nearly 1½ million people to New York's Metropolitan Museum of Art in the spring of 1979, to see masterpieces that had never before left Egypt.

Museums also vied to obtain pieces of increasing rarity. Soon after the Metropolitan Museum acquired this sixth-century B.C. Attic ceramic calyx krater the Italian government claimed that it had been smuggled out of Italy. Soaring prices in the art market encouraged flagrant violation of antique-export laws and the production of counterfeits. Reputable institutions and dealers worked hard to reduce illegal traffic in art works.

The Metropolitan Museum of Art, Bequest of Joseph H. Durkee, Gift of Darius Ogden Mills, and Gift of C. Ruxton Love, by Exchange, 1972.

Photo by Gianfranco Gorgoni, *courtesy*, the Estate of Robert Smithson, John Weber Gallery, New York

Some contemporary artists turned to explorations of concept and scale. The 1970 earth sculpture (*above*) by Robert Smithson reached some 400 feet into the Great Salt Lake in Utah. It was a 1,500-foot spiral jetty composed of black rock, white salt crystals, and yellowish earth in a setting of water colored red by the presence of algae. (*Below*) Designer Frank Gehry indulged sculptural whimsy with compressed cardboard to create furniture that questions the boxlike character of conventional tables and chairs.

DIVERSION

Photo by Burton Wilson

In the "radical" 1960s, public expression of individuality had appealed to many young people. (*Above*) Costumes worn as street clothing, impromptu sidewalk performances, long hair and beards, and other social gestures were evidences of a teenage generation trying to define itself during the period of the Beatles, civil rights protests, and student demonstrations. In the 1970s, "private" activities such as video games and solving Rubik's Cube® (*below*) were popular. The cube—a manipulative puzzle that required arranging colored patches on each face in a stated pattern—was a major fad. Young people with an almost intuitive sense of visual pattern, like the nine-year-old shown here, proved to be speed champions in solving the puzzle.

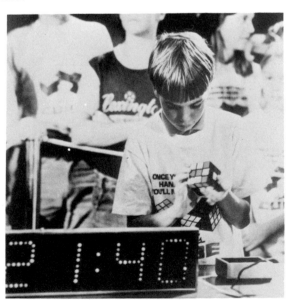

Rubik's Cube® is a registered trademark of CBS, Inc., and is used solely by its permission.

Courtesy, RCA

Home entertainment centered largely around the television set. Video-discs—the television equivalent of LP records—were introduced with much fanfare in the early 1980s. Within four years, production of discs and players had virtually ceased, for the public seemed more interested in rival videotape cassette systems. Videotape allows viewers to record programs at will, to erase and reuse tapes, and to make the equivalent of home movies using a simplified video camera. This disc system offered no such versatility.

THE ART AND SCIENCE OF MEDICINE

Medical science made significant advances in equipment, in mass treatment, and in dealing with the public and private aspects of an individual's accepting treatment for serious disease. Multimillion-dollar equipment received much publicity, especially new devices for visual investigation inside the body. Computer-assisted tomography (CAT-scans) achieved new precision and sophistication in X-ray examinations of patients. Nuclear magnetic resonance (NMR) equipment achieved similar results without subjecting patients to X-ray radiation. However, perhaps the most widely adopted and useful new tool was the laser scalpel, shown *below* in use for an eye operation. A laser is a variable-power, concentrated light beam that can be controlled with almost infinite precision. Among thousands of tasks, lasers can be used to map the surface of planets, to drill holes through diamonds, or to cut delicately to the depth of a single cell or tissue-layer. Because the surgical laser injures much less tissue than a conventional blade scalpel, there is less bleeding and potential pain. Many operations that once were full-scale operating room procedures can now be accomplished with only a local anaesthetic in a clinic or even in a doctor's office.

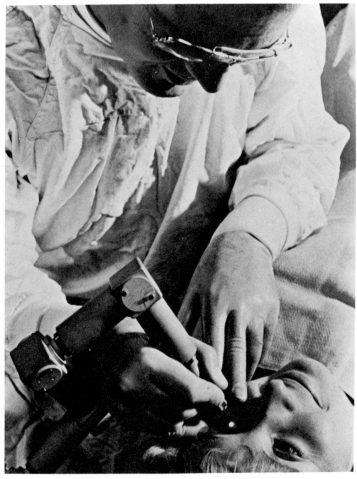

Courtesy, AT&T Corporate Archive

Improved research and procedures at federal disease control centers make it possible to deal with large-scale problems such as potential epidemics more rapidly and efficiently. (*Above*) Millions of people had to be inoculated in 1975–1976 as a preventive measure against a predicted outbreak of swine influenza. Jet injectors that spray vaccine through the pores without breaking the skin were used to inoculate large numbers of people in a short period at stations throughout the country. Public awareness of the value in dealing immediately with serious disease was increased as a number of celebrities made public their conditions and treatment. (*Below*) Mrs. Gerald Ford tosses a football to her husband, the ex-president, as she leaves the hospital after a mammillectomy to remove cancerous tissue. Several other prominent women acknowledged undergoing similar surgery, helping to dispel the unreasonable secrecy and shame associated with breast cancer.

ART AND BUSINESS IN RELIGION

Following a tradition established during the days of radio, telecasts of
local church services were an early feature of stations in many American
cities. In the 1970s, nationwide TV evangelism found an audience that
grew steadily into hundreds of thousands of viewers who donated millions of dollars in contributions. Most such programs were produced on
videotape in a TV studio or a church-owned broadcast center and were
distributed to a network of subscriber stations for broadcast on a regular
schedule. The most famous evangelists often could arrange for live
telecasts and recordings of mass revivals and faith rallies held in major
cities.

Photo by Craig Brewer

Photo by Lautman

Old, established churches and denominations also experienced a growth of interest and attendance. This is the congregation at Washington Cathedral, Mount Saint Alban, Washington, D. C., on Easter morning 1976. In some urban neighborhoods, the mission of the local church— and even the language of its services—changed with shifts in the economic status and ethnic heritage of the local population.

UPI/Bettmann

Of the several cults and religious sects that appeared in the United States during the 1970s, by far the largest and most publicized was the Unification Church, founded by the Reverend Sun Myung Moon of Korea. The church proselytized energetically among teenagers and young adults, had compelling indoctrination sessions, and required that followers donate most or all of their assets. In this photograph, the Rev. Moon and his wife (at left) officiate at the largest mass wedding in history: a ceremony in Madison Square Garden, New York, July 1, 1978, that married 2,200 couples. Many of the brides were Korean young women brought to America by the church. In the early 1980s, the Rev. Moon was found guilty of not paying income taxes on church funds diverted to his private use and was sentenced to jail.

8.

SPORTS AND RECREATION

Intended to test and celebrate the athletic achievement of the individual, in the post–World War II period the Olympic Games have increasingly been the focus of nationalism as various countries—especially the United States and the U.S.S.R.—have publicized the number of medals won by their athletes, implying that a given social-political system is somehow responsible for excellence in sports. The summer Olympic Games of 1968, held in Mexico City, saw the injection of an overt political note (*see photo below*) for the first time since the Nazis had tried to turn the 1936 Berlin games into a propaganda spectacular. Political gesture and action have since repeatedly plagued the Olympics. In 1972, demands from black African nations caused the exclusion of Rhodesia from the games on the ground that its racist policies were not in accord with the Olympic spirit. More terrifying was the assassination of eleven Israeli Olympic athletes by Arab terrorists at Munich. In 1980, Canada, West Germany, Japan, and fifty-eight other nations joined the United States in boycotting the summer Olympic Games in Moscow, to protest Russia's invasion of Afghanistan. In retaliation, sixteen Soviet-bloc and sympathetic nations refused to participate in the 1984 summer games in Los Angeles. As a result, finding a permanent, politically neutral site for the Olympics began to be seriously discussed.

Two black Americans raise their arms to salute Black Power during the playing of the national anthem after receiving gold and silver medals in the 200-meter run at the 1968 Olympics in Mexico City. The black-gloved clenched fist was a gesture of defiance to white America adopted by many militant black groups during the civil rights activism of the 1960s. The two athletes, Tommie Smith (center) and Juan Carlos, were expelled from the American team. Many felt this an overreaction to an overreported incident, especially since there was no action or press comment when a white American medal winner kept his cap on during the anthem a few days later.

AP/Wide World Photos

AP/Wide World Photos

Mark Spitz breaks his own world record, set earlier the same day, in the 200-meter butterfly event in the 1972 Olympic Swimming Trials in Chicago. At the Munich games later that summer, the twenty-two-year-old Spitz won four individual gold medals, setting a new Olympic record time in each event, and three team gold medals—the greatest total ever won by an individual.

Dorothy Hamill of the United States (center), women's figure-skating gold medal winner at the 1976 Winter Olympics, held in Innsbruck, Austria. The silver medal was won by Diane De Leeuw of Holland (left), the bronze by Christine Errath of East Germany (right). In this same year, Hamill became the champion woman figure skater in the United States for the third time and also won the world championship.

UPI/Bettmann

Bruce Jenner and a Polish competitor, Ryszard Skowronek, in a 110-meter hurdles heat of the decathlon in the 1976 summer Olympics at Montreal. Jenner established a new record point-total in the decathlon to become the ninth American to win the competition since 1912, when it was introduced in the modern games.

UPI/Bettmann

PERSONAL BESTS

Despite President Jimmy Carter's decision to boycott the 1980 Moscow Olympics in protest against Soviet action in Afghanistan, earlier American triumphs in the Olympics and the increased popularity of spectator sports during the 1960s and 1970s helped spark a great growth in individual participation. Hundreds of thousands took up exercising or playing sports on a regular basis to gain the health benefits of physical fitness and the satisfaction of achieving the very best one could do in a chosen physical activity.

Jogging quickly became the most popular individual activity, largely because it could be done almost anywhere, alone or with others, without special equipment. Suburban roads and city streets and parks—this is the pathway around the reservoir in New York City's Central Park—become crowded with people getting cardiovascular exercise before or after work.

Photo © Jim Anderson 1978/Woodfin Camp & Associates

Marathons and other long-distance races for amateurs gained in popularity during the 1970s, probably as a result of the growth in jogging. In 1983, the eighty-sixth Boston marathon and the fifth New York marathon each attracted thousands of entrants, including many from foreign countries. Both races were 26 miles, 385 yards long and were won in slightly more than 2 hours, 8 minutes in the men's class, and 2 hours, 27 minutes in the women's class. These runners are in the first (1979) New York marathon.

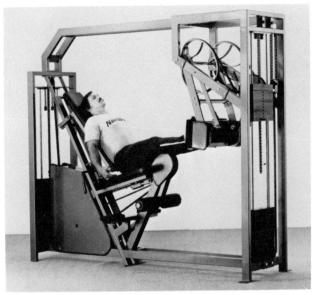

Courtesy, Nautilus Sports/Medical Industries, Inc.

Many Americans found it easiest to exercise in the atmosphere and with the facilities and professional direction offered by a health club or gymnasium. To satisfy public demand, such organizations grew from a few mats and calisthenics sessions to offer a broad variety of classes with facilities that included swimming pools, saunas, massage rooms, and a great array of equipment. Multifunction exercise machines such as those shown here are far more effective and versatile than the barbells and Indian clubs of earlier years.

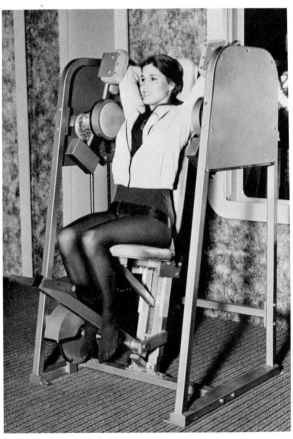

Courtesy, Nautilus Sports/Medical Industries, Inc.

The number of Americans sixty-five and older increases by about 500,000 each year. As a group they are "younger" than in previous decades because a significant number have taken up exercising and other physical activities. They have found that physical fitness is accompanied by increased mental alertness and a sustained interest in remaining active participants in life.

Calisthenics in the pool—aquacises—are easier and more fun, but no less effective, than dry-land exercises.

Courtesy, Century Village West, Boca Raton, Florida

Calisthenics in a retirement community in the Southwest.

Adult-size tricycles are popular at this retirement park in St. Petersburg, Florida. Easier to handle than two-wheelers, they are not only an excellent way to exercise but can be used for light shopping.

Courtesy, Florida Department of Commerce, Division of Tourism

RECREATION: IN THE ELEMENTS

Like many other recreational activities, powerboating expanded greatly
in the 1970s, which created an increase in water skiing. Only a small
percentage of skiers ever master the use of a single ski, like this en-
thusiast on Lake Tenkiller, Oklahoma.

Courtesy, Oklahoma Tourism and Recreation Department

Steve Wilkings/WIND SURF Magazine

Windsurfing married a sail to a surfboard and became a standard water sport in just a few years. This is United States champion Matt Schweitzer, along the California coast. Similar equipment is widely used by young sailors on freshwater lakes where good breezes are common.

UPI/Bettmann

Hang gliding, mountain climbing, sky diving, and other activities for the intrepid also showed a surge in popularity in the 1970s. This eighty-pound hang glider soaring off Lookout Mountain, near Golden, Colorado, is the Icarus V. Its swept-wing design looks more like traditional aircraft than the more common kite-shaped and double-batwing hang gliders.

The public appetite for watching daredevil feats while sitting comfortably in front of their television sets was exploited by professional stunt man Evel Knievel. A great publicity buildup preceded his attempt in September 1974 to jump 1,700 feet across the Snake River Canyon at Twin Falls, Idaho, on a steam-rocket motorcycle. (*Below*) Knievel prepares to climb into the streamlined capsule of his Skycar. The Skycar did not reach the other side. A safety parachute dropped Knievel and his cycle to the river below.

AP/Wide World Photos   UPI/Bettmann

FOUR HOOVES: FAST, FURIOUS

As a three-year-old, the thoroughbred Secretariat became a racing legend in 1973 and was named Horse of the Year. The first horse to win the Triple Crown (Kentucky Derby, Preakness Stakes, Belmont Stakes) in twenty-five years, he set record times at the Derby and at Belmont that have never been equaled. He is seen here in a workout with jockey Ron Turcotte.

AP/Wide World Photos

Courtesy, Texas State Department of Highways—Travel and Information Division

In the Southwest, rodeoing takes the place of racing or dressage. Riding an agitated Brahma bull like the one shown here in Austin, Texas, for as long as thirty seconds can provide a real heart-stopping thrill even for spectators. Other standard events at such annual rodeos as the Southwestern Fat Stock Show and Rodeo in Fort Worth include riding bucking broncos, steer wrestling (bulldogging), and roping and tying.

GROWTH SPORTS

Tennis participation, attendance, and equipment sales have increased every year since the late 1960s, and professional tennis has become a major money sport. Women's tennis received a great boost in September 1973 from a cleverly built-up $100,000 "Battle of the Sexes." Bobby Riggs, twice United States men's singles champion and Wimbledon champion in 1939, mocked the abilities of women players widely and issued a challenge to the reigning women's champion, Billie Jean King, with the insulting claim that a fifty-five-year-old man should have no trouble beating a woman twenty-five years younger. Mrs. King beat Riggs as anticipated, and the publicity accompanying the match was worth millions in promoting women's tennis. She retired from active play in 1983, having won the United States women's singles, doubles, and mixed doubles championships four times each, and the Wimbledon women's singles championship six times.

UPI/Bettmann

Courtesy, New York Cosmos

The number of professional teams in the North American Soccer League nearly doubled, from eight to fourteen, in the decade of 1972–1982. In the same period many high schools and colleges, especially in the eastern United States, added soccer to their athletic programs. The foremost sport of Europe and South America, soccer gained attention and popularity in this country when the spectacular Brazilian player Pelé (Edson Arantes do Nascimento) came out of retirement in 1975 to join the New York Cosmos with a $7 million contract. Here, Pelé is number 10, sixth from the left.

THE NATIONAL GAME

Major league baseball had expanded twice in the 1960s to two six-team divisions, east and west, in both the American and National leagues. The total of twenty-four teams remained unchanged, but attendance grew in the next decade by more than 55 percent. In 1982, almost 44,600,000 fans paid to attend major league games, while millions more watched on television. The decade also saw the first job action for players' benefits (*opposite*), the first multimillion-dollar contracts for star players, and a new home run king, Hank Aaron, who reached a lifetime total of 755 regular-season home runs, forty-one more than Babe Ruth's long-standing record.

Ed Kranepool (right) gives Tug McGraw a champagne shampoo as they celebrate the New York Mets' victory in the fifth game with the Baltimore Orioles to take the 1969 World Series title. Mets fans were astounded and delighted: since 1962, the year it was created, the team had never finished above ninth place in the National League.

UPI/Bettmann

UPI/Bettmann

(*Above*) The new scoreboard in San Francisco's Candlestick Park tells the big baseball story in April 1972. Players in both leagues refused to play at the opening of the season in a protest over the size of pension fund contributions from team owners. (*Right*) Two Cincinnati Reds players leave spring training camp in Florida to begin the strike. It was the first such action in the history of the game. By the time the dispute was settled, thirteen days later, eighty-four games had been cancelled.

UPI/Bettmann

BASKETBALL, THE GAME OF AGILE GIANTS

Both college and professional basketball prospered in the 1970s. In addition to being the tallest athletes in the country, by 1984 basketball stars were among the highest paid. For some, the publicity gained as players was a decided asset in building subsequent careers.

New York Knickerbocker Walt Frazier (number 10) outreaches Jack Marin of the Baltimore Bullets in a 1972 National Basketball Association playoff game. The Knicks went on to the championship series, where they lost to the Los Angeles Lakers, but beat them the following year. Knick player number 24, in the background, is Bill Bradley. Six years later he was elected United States senator from New Jersey.

AP/Wide World Photos

AP/Wide World Photos

With this shot in a December 1980 game in Inglewood, California, Kareem Abdul-Jabbar becomes the fifth man in basketball history to score 25,000 points. Born Lewis Ferdinand Alcindor, Jr., he was a star player at Power Memorial in New York City and at UCLA, before changing his name upon conversion to Islam during his professional career.

FALL IS FOOTBALL

From a game of local college rivalry, football has grown to be America's major infatuation on fall weekends and one of its biggest sports businesses. Far more fans attend football games than any other sport, and the television audience is much larger. Elaborate pregame and halftime shows turn the sports event into a ceremonial spectacular. Here, some 81,000 fans watch opening ceremonies at a Sugar Bowl game in New Orleans. Some figures reveal the dimensions of football's popularity: 146 major college and professional stadiums have capacities from 25,000 to 110,000; more than half of these accommodate 50,000 or more people. More than 150 games are played each weekend of the season. There are nineteen major postseason college bowl games for interconference championships. The biggest game of all is the professional postseason Super Bowl, begun in 1967. The television audience for Super Bowl XVIII in January 1984 was more than 110 million.

UPI/Bettmann

VACATIONING IN AMERICA

Taking a vacation became more affordable from 1972 to 1982, when per capita annual income almost tripled, from $4,500 to $11,000. Travel to foreign countries increased enormously, but vacation travel within the United States grew even more. The National Park system had to cope with an increasing number of visitors, to the point of overcapacity each year in the most popular locations. Many states and municipalities invested heavily in improving and publicizing their vacation facilities, for annual profits from tourists and vacationers can amount to many millions of dollars. People traveled farther to spend more, at both public and privately operated attractions, than ever before. Others invested in increasingly expensive and luxurious equipment for camping, boating, and other leisure-time and vacation activities.

Courtesy, Washington State Travel

Natural wonders are among America's most popular attractions. This is Dry Falls, near the Grand Coulee Dam, in the Sun Lakes (Washington) State Park. The enormous eroded cliffs are evidence of a cataract 100 times greater than Niagara that was formed when retreating glaciers blocked the Columbia River during the Pleistocene epoch, almost 2 million years ago.

Courtesy, Wyoming Travel Commission

Snowmobiles were allowed in the national parks for the first time in the 1970s. This group is at Yellowstone National Park in Wyoming. While immensely popular with enthusiasts, snowmobiles are considered a major nuisance by those who prefer quiet and unmarked beauty in a winter scene.

Photo by Mike DuBose, *courtesy*, Knoxville World's Fair

Fairs of all sizes, particularly the world's fairs, at which many countries can display their technological, industrial, and cultural accomplishments, are perennial favorites with vacationers. The site of the 1982 World's Fair in Knoxville, Tennessee, was dominated by the Sunsphere —a 266-foot structure topped by a five-level sphere encased in glass impregnated with 24-karat gold dust—and a man-made, three-acre "Waters of the World" lake.

States that border on the Atlantic or Pacific ocean, or on the Gulf of Mexico, are especially popular with vacationers. On the East Coast, the seasonal flow north and south is especially marked.

Ocean beaches like these at Ogunquit, Maine, are popular vacation spots to avoid the summer heat. The rocky, undeveloped coast contrasts greatly with the most popular beaches in the south.

Photo by John Norton, *courtesy*, Maine Dept. of Commerce & Industry

Photo by John Norton, *courtesy*, Maine Dept. of Commerce & Industry

Lobster pots, fishing and pleasure boats, and pine woods are characteristic of the Maine seacoast.

Development is a major characteristic of much of the Atlantic coast in Florida. The number of vacation hotels along the luxurious white sands of Miami Beach mushroomed in the 1920s, were largely replaced in the 1950s, and by the 1970s had transformed the isthmus into an almost unbroken line of modern establishments catering to tens of thousands every winter.

© Walt Disney Productions

Walt Disney World, opened in 1971, attracts a steady stream of visitors all year long. The once seasonal tourist business in the Orlando area has been transformed.

Courtesy, Cessna Aircraft Co.

(*Above*) Increasing affluence has made it possible for some middle-income families to own or lease a small airplane, making vacation spots easily accessible even from long distances.

(*Below*) A far greater number of people could afford the pleasures of a power boat than a small plane. Conventional-hull power boats are common along the coasts and on the lakes and inland waterways of Florida, but exploring the shallow waters of the Everglades requires a flat-bottom design such as this.

Courtesy, Florida Department of Commerce, Division of Tourism

9.

MUSIC
AND
ENTERTAINMENT

The growth in cultural and leisure activities that accompanied the increasing affluence of the previous decade continued well into the 1972–1982 period. Mass-media entertainment and pop stars attracted the largest audiences, but classical music, opera, dance, drama, and similar activities also drew new millions of people to performances throughout the country. The number of significant symphony orchestras increased by more than one-half, to 162. New museums were created; established institutions expanded; and new cultural organizations and facilities were established. The John F. Kennedy Center for the Performing Arts, in Washington, D. C., was one such facility. At the inauguration of the Opera House in September 1971 (*below*), a prestigious audience was invited to hear a symphonic mass composed and conducted by Leonard Bernstein. (The exterior of the Center is shown on page 108.)

AP/Wide World Photos

ONSTAGE

Photo by Louis Mélançon

Grand opera regained a popularity it had not enjoyed since the days of Caruso. By 1982 there were forty-seven opera companies in the United States with annual budgets of $500,000 or more. Newly staged productions by the Metropolitan Opera Company of New York—which had moved into a new opera house in Lincoln Center in 1966—were widely acclaimed. Here, the great dramatic soprano Leontyne Price (kneeling, center) sings the title role in Verdi's *Aida*. Price, along with Grace Bumbry and Shirley Verette, is one of the few black women to sing lead roles in American opera productions, a distinction first achieved at the Met by Marian Anderson, in 1955.

Photo by Sy Friedman, Zodiac Photographers

Rock opera appeared on Broadway in 1971 in the form of the enormously popular *Jesus Christ Superstar*. The stage production, with Jeff Fenholt in the role of Jesus, was developed from a hit record album that married rock music to the antiestablishment attitudes and religious-mystical yearnings of many young people of the time.

Courtesy, Harkness Ballet Foundation, Photo by Bil Leidersdorf

Ballet attracted a growing following, as witnessed by the formation of such new companies as the Houston Ballet and the Dance Theatre of Harlem (1968), the Pittsburgh Ballet (1970), and the Feld Ballet of New York (1974). This early 1970s production of *Night Song* is by New York's Harkness Ballet, founded in 1964 to afford its students an opportunity to perform.

THE BEATLES

The first white group to make rock music popular with the enormous audience of teenagers around the world was the Beatles, four boys from Liverpool, England. From their first international hit, "Love Me, Do," in 1962, they attracted unequaled adulation from millions of fans. Their music grew to incorporate many other strains that appealed to and influenced both audiences and other performers: rhythms and motifs absorbed during a tour of India, drug imagery, anti–middle class social comment, electronic sound, and fantasy. Although they disbanded in 1970 to pursue separate careers, their following grew to include large numbers of adults and less popularly oriented musicians.

The Beatles in performance (left to right): John Lennon, Paul McCartney, George Harrison, Ringo Starr.

AP/Wide World Photos

AP/Wide World Photos

Beatle John Lennon was shot to death in New York City by a deranged attacker on December 10, 1980. Spontaneous memorial demonstrations like this candlelight vigil in Los Angeles occurred around the world in the days immediately following. Lennon's work was carried on by his widow, Yoko Ono, with whom he had collaborated on several songs and albums in the years just before his death.

UPI/Bettmann

In seeking an alternative culture, some young people were strongly attracted by the exotic aspects of various Oriental sects. This Hare Krishna group in Minneapolis has adopted the dress, shaved heads, ascetic discipline, and practice of public chanting and dancing to raise money that are part of an Indian faith.

ROCK: HARD, DRUG, AND MILD

The now-common outdoor concerts for huge gatherings of teenagers began with the first festival at Woodstock, New York, in 1969. Almost 400,000 people jammed a thirty-five-acre site with grossly inadequate facilities and organization for a delirious weekend of rock and blues music, alcohol and marijuana, and uninhibited interaction. At the end, almost all agreed that they were exhausted and had had the time of their lives.

AP/Wide World Photos

A dozen years after Woodstock, top rock groups such as the Rolling Stones attracted audiences with aggressive, highly amplified, repetitive music. Here the Stones perform before an audience of 90,000 in Philadelphia's John F. Kennedy Stadium. Left to right, they are: Ron Wood, Mick Jagger, Charlie Watts, and Keith Richards.

AP/Wide World Photos

Rock festivals immediately following Woodstock were marked with increasing lawlessness and violence. At Altamont, California, in 1970, members of the Hell's Angels—an outlaw motorcycle club hired for $500 worth of beer to keep order—hauled a spectator onstage and mauled him. Here, performer Mick Jagger reacts to the beginning of the incident. There was also a fatal shooting in the audience. Later in the decade, violence was confined to the music and onstage dramatizations at most concerts.

Janis Joplin, probably the most popular female rock vocalist, typified the destructive link between rock music and the drug culture. A regular user of both alcohol and hard drugs, she died of a drug overdose in 1970, at the age of twenty-seven.

UPI/Bettmann

Columbia Pictures

Rock music was inevitably watered down and gentrified to appeal to a middle-class, mass-media audience. The Monkees were a group formed to appear in a television situation comedy of the same name about teenage musicians. Both the music and the comedy were mild. The series ran for fifty-eight episodes from 1966 to 1973, moving successively to all three major networks. The performers—located by trade-journal ads in Los Angeles—at first pantomimed to the music of others, but eventually played on the program and recorded several albums.

THE KING IS DEAD

Elvis Presley, who started as a gospel-singing child in church, transformed country music with a hard beat into rock 'n' roll, beginning with "Mystery Train" in 1954 and "Heartbreak Hotel," his first major rhythm-and-blues hit, in 1956. Here, he shows forty-year-old heaviness, in 1976, but his audiences were large and enthusiastic, as they had been for two decades.

AP/Wide World Photos

UPI/Bettmann

Presley's death in August 1977 of an apparent heart attack shocked and saddened millions who had grown from their teens to mid-life along with him. His home has become a museum and his grave almost a shrine, visited by grieving fans each year on the anniversary of his death.

COUNTRY-AND-WESTERN MUSIC

What was once dismissed as mountain, hillbilly, and cowboy music grew to be a multimillion-dollar entertainment industry in the mid-1960s, and the growth continued in the 1970s. Hits by top country-and-western singers and songwriters began "crossing over" from the country sales charts to the pop-music listings, which reflected a much larger audience. Two television series, "The Beverly Hillbillies" and "Hee Haw," were based on "country" themes. Country music specials and award programs were broadcast in prime time. Interest in early, precommercial country music sparked development of a widely popular revival style called bluegrass. At the center of this growth from the beginning was the radio—and since the late 1950s, television—program "Grand Ole Opry." Starting in a small studio of station WSM in Nashville, Tennessee, in 1925, the program moved to larger facilities and finally to its own modern theater, production center, and tourist attraction, Opryland U.S.A. Paralleling this growth was the emergence of a music publishing industry which, along with the Opry, made Nashville the country music capital of the world. Appearing on an Opry broadcast marked a performer's arrival at the very top of his field and virtually assured him of continued success. Many, like Minnie Pearl and Roy Acuff, at the center stage microphones (*below*), became regular performers on the Opry for decades.

Courtesy, Nashville Chamber of Commerce

AP/Wide World Photos

While several black men have achieved stardom as jazz or rhythm-and-blues singers, Charley Pride was the first to be recognized as a top country music performer. His hit album, "Country Charley Pride," and his first appearance on Grand Ole Opry, both in 1967, signaled the emergence of a major talent in the field, one whose career grew rapidly in the next decade.

Dolly Parton was named Female Singer of the Year by the Country Music Association in 1975 and again in 1976. Her career was established with regular performances on local radio and television at the age of ten. She made her first records and Grand Ole Opry appearance three years later. In 1974 she became a solo act, after seven years with Porter Wagoner, and soon was a pop-music as well as a country star. Her range of musical skills and her dramatic work in various movies and television productions have begun to change her public image from a bosomy, bleached blonde to that of a mature performer.

UPI/Bettmann

FOLK REVIVAL

The diversity of interest in American music included great enthusiasm for traditional as well as modern urban folk songs. While professional performers appeared in concerts and on television and made records, amateurs and semiprofessionals found performance opportunities in a variety of local and regional festivals and contests. This group is at the White Springs Folk Festival in Florida.

Courtesy, Florida Department of Commerce, Division of Tourism

James J. Kriegsmann

The rhythm-and-blues music of black America evolved in two directions: rock 'n' roll, which came to be dominated by white musicians, and a sophisticated modern form called soul music, which remained the province of black performers. The top soul group of the 1970s was the Supremes, who recorded for Motown, a variant of the nickname "motor city" for Detroit.

DISCO

Originally, a discotheque was a small nightclub for dancing to recorded
music. In the 1970s it became a large dance area with lasers, psychedelic
light and sound effects, mixed-media displays, and highly amplified,
electronically manipulated music, all of which created a fantasy environment. This is opening night in 1978 at Xenon, a new $2-million dis-
cotheque in New York City. Many of its spectacular features were
created by a specialist in science fiction movie effects.

UPI/Bettmann

Americans spent more time watching television each week in the 1970s than in any other activity except working and sleeping. While many programs repeated familiar patterns, there was increasing diversity. Social comment was combined with situation comedy (*below*); public television attracted a significant portion of the audience with a range of excellent cultural, informational, and dramatic presentations; and sports coverage increased, both for the established major sports and for those gaining in popularity, such as tennis, soccer, and golf. Two- and three-hour "specials" on a single theme became common and the "mini-series" emerged—the dramatization of a book, typically presented in three to eight closely scheduled episodes of 90- or 120-minute length. Many of the most popular network series lived on after the production of new episodes ended, sold for reruns—often with new titles—in seemingly endless repetitions on local stations. Toward the end of the decade, the pattern of a hit movie generating a television series was reversed when several long-run television series became the basis of one or more full-length theatrical motion pictures. A notable example was "Star Trek" (see page 218).

Courtesy, Tandem Productions

True storyline innovation appeared in Norman Lear's "All in the Family," which ran in prime evening network time for nine seasons, beginning in 1971. Inspired by a British working-class series, it used blue-collar family situations to examine racism, male chauvinism, abortion, and other social topics. A current of comedy accompanied probing, although indirect, social comment. The central character, who has become an American stereotype, was the bigoted factory foreman Archie Bunker, played by Carroll O'Connor (right). Other members of his family were (left to right) his wife Edith (Jean Stapleton), daughter Gloria (Sally Struthers), and liberal son-in-law Mike "Meathead" Stivic (Rob Reiner).

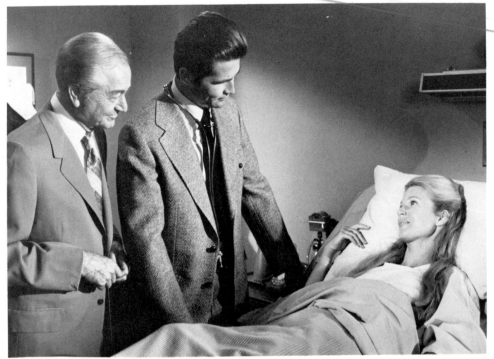

Hospitals and doctors, staples of daytime soap operas, have also been the focus of several prime-time evening series. The most popular from 1969 to 1976 (and still widely seen in reruns) was "Marcus Welby, M.D." Robert Young (left) starred in the title role, resolving crises and guiding the career of young doctor Steve Kiley (James Brolin, center). The patients and traumas were new each week.

Telly Savalas (left) played a hard-boiled New York City police lieutenant in the 110 episodes of "Kojak" produced from 1973 to 1977. To distinguish his character from those in other police series, Savalas shaved his head bald, wore fancy vests, and sucked on lollipops—presumably to keep from smoking.

Courtesy, The New York Public Library Picture Collection

Copyright British Broadcasting Corporation 1972

One of the finest jobs of describing our national development was done by a transplanted Englishman, Alistair Cooke, perennial host of dramas on the public television series "Masterpiece Theater." His own thirteen-part "America," presented in the 1972–1973 season, traced the country's growth across three centuries, from wilderness to industrialized, computerized superpower.

London Weekend Television

Of the many excellent British productions that have been the mainstay of public television's "Masterpiece Theater," none has been more popular than "Upstairs, Downstairs." From 1972 to 1974 (and in subsequent repeat broadcasts), Americans saw about a third of the original seventy-five episodes dramatizing class interaction and social change from turn-of-the-century Edwardian England to the eve of World War II. The central figure was the upstairs maid, Rose, played by Jean Marsh (left); downstairs was ruled by Cook, played by Angela Baddeley.

In an unprecedented 250 episodes from 1972 to 1983, "M*A*S*H" evolved from raw, near-slapstick army comedy to serious human concerns couched in gentle humor, and both explicit and implicit protests against the insanity of war. Laid in a Mobile Army Surgical Hospital unit during the Korean War of the 1950s, it actually spoke to the concerns of a post–Vietnam audience that grew in size each season. Stars throughout the series were Alan Alda (standing, right center) as Captain Benjamin Franklin "Hawkeye" Pierce, a surgeon, and Loretta Swit as Major Margaret "Hotlips" Houlihan, chief of nurses. Other regular characters in many episodes were the commanding officer, Colonel Sherman Potter (Harry Morgan, seated), the chaplain, Father John Mulcahy (William Christopher, standing, left), and Captain B. J. Hunnicutt (Mike Farrell, center), also a surgeon.

Courtesy, New York Public Library Picture Collection

For three seasons, beginning in 1976, "The Muppet Show" delighted both children and adults as no puppet program had done since "Kukla, Fran, and Ollie" in the late 1940s and early 1950s. The variety of characters, construction, and manipulative techniques of the Muppets both rejuvenated and revolutionized puppetry as popular entertainment. The nominal star was Kermit the Frog, alter ego of Muppet originator Jim Henson, but Miss Piggy—the creation of long-time Muppeteer Frank Oz—bulldozed her way to world stardom with a saccharine charm that continually slipped to expose a whim of iron and a physically militant feminism that could crush armies. The series was produced in England, where it was also immensely popular, because Henson could not find financing in the United States at the beginning. There have since also been three feature-length Muppet movies, with more likely.

© Henson Associates, Inc., 1982

4E   71

ALEX HALEY'S BOYHOOD HOME

Will Palmer, a prominent Henning businessman,
built this house in 1918-19. Palmer's grandson
Alex Haley lived here from 1921 to 1929 and
later spent many summers with his grandparents.
It was on the porch that he heard the stories
told by his grandmother and
inspired him to write his
ize-winning book Roo
nericans watched
elevision adaptation
'ear

UPI/Bettmann

A landmark in the development of the mini-series was the twelve-hour saga "Roots," first presented in 1977 on eight consecutive nights to a record-breaking audience. It traced the heritage of millions of black Americans, from capture and slave trading in Africa to importation in pre– and post–Revolutionary times and the life of subsequent generations here.

Alex Haley (*above*), author of the book from which the television epic was drawn, was a professional writer who mixed fact and fiction to create an autobiography of a racial minority. Born in 1921, Haley heard many of the stories and incidents woven into *Roots* from family members and visitors to his home in Henning, Tennessee. The house was made a state historical site soon after the success of the book and television program.

"Dallas," begun in 1978, deals with ruthlessness and treachery in business, sex, family, and society. J. R. Ewing, played by Larry Hagman (right), is the chief unscrupulous rotter in this series that has attracted a large audience who thrive on seamy melodrama with artificial Texan accents.

Feature films have been a major part of television programing from the early 1950s. The war films and middle-aged-hero westerns of John Wayne were especially popular on television in the 1970s. Wayne, who died in 1979, made more than 150 movies in his career. Here he is seen in the star role in "The Green Berets," a 1968 saga of Special Forces personnel in Southeast Asia which he also directed. Like most Wayne war films, it championed the military as faultless and invincible protectors of the American way of life.

While television began to finance low-budget, made-for-TV movies to fill the demand for features, Hollywood discovered that there was money to be made with expensive films crammed with special effects or featuring a very few top stars. Science fiction films burst into spectacular success in 1977 with "Star Wars," a classic space opera with easy-to-identify heroes, extraterrestrial villains, battles beyond the wildest imagination of a video-game devotee, and dazzling visual effects produced by computer-controlled equipment. Here, Luke Skywalker (Mark Hamill) looks over the two most personable robots in movie history, the shiny R2-D2, and the short, squat C-3-PO. The trio and their cohorts have returned in two subsequent films of what may become a twelve-feature saga.

The adventures of the star ship U. S. S. *Enterprise* in the twenty-second century had been depicted in the seventy-nine television episodes of "Star Trek" from 1966 to 1969. Then devotees had to search out reruns to maintain their close identification with the lead characters (left to right): ship's doctor Leonard McCoy (DeForrest Kelley), commander James Kirk (William Shatner), and first officer Spock (Leonard Nimoy), an emotionless, supremely logical being from the planet Vulcan. After a decade in the television wilderness, joyous fans flocked to "Star Trek: The Movie" in 1979, and to two feature-length sequels in the next few years.

The first modern space spectacular did not have wild battles, encounters with lurid extraterrestrials, or other elements dear to sci-fi audiences. Instead, "2001: A Space Odyssey," released in 1968, was a serious effort by writer Arthur C. Clarke and director Stanley Kubrick to examine in dramatic form the past and future evolution of human beings in the context of predictable space technology. However, the most memorable character was HAL, a speaking computer that attempted to seize control of a space ship from humans it considered inferior in intelligence. Originally released in super-widescreen format, the film tended to envelop young audiences in a space-drafting experience that obliterated its ostensible message. A sequel, "2010," was produced sixteen years later.

Courtesy, Metro-Goldwyn-Mayer, Inc.

In "The Exorcist," the horror of human beings caught up in the eternal battle between good and evil took on new dimensions of melodramatic realism. The book by William Blatty told of the struggle to free the soul of a child possessed by a demon. It sold more than 5 million copies, and the 1973 movie version made more money than any film in almost a decade.

© 1973 Warner Bros. Inc. and Hoya Productions, Inc.

The exquisite pleasure of being terrified while in the safety of a movie seat drew people in unprecedented numbers around the world to see "Jaws." Released in 1975, the story of a marauding shark and its victims became the first movie in history to earn more than $100 million.

United Artists

Sylvester Stallone gave new life to the always popular theme of the underdog who wins against all odds, in "Rocky." The film won Academy Awards in 1976 for best picture and best direction, and spawned three sequels. In addition to starring as a boxer who would not give up, Stallone wrote the screenplay; his girl friend was played by Talia Shire.

© 1976 Warner Bros. Inc. and Wildwood Enterprises, Inc.

In the second half of the 1970s, several movies turned a probing eye on political and social problems of the immediately preceding years. They were unusual in their factual directness and their only slightly understated criticism of certain aspects of American society. "All the President's Men" (1976) dealt with the Watergate scandal (see pages 12–17) and was based on the best-selling book of that title by Carl Bernstein and Bob Woodward. Dustin Hoffman and Robert Redford (*above*) played the two reporters whose investigative articles helped win the 1973 Pulitzer Prize for meritorious public service for their newspaper, the *Washington Post*. "Coming Home" (*below*), released in 1978, three years after the end of the Vietnam War (see Chapter 2), was one of the first pictures to humanize the problems that veterans faced, in a way that attracted a large audience. Jane Fonda played a hospital volunteer who became romantically involved with a permanently disabled war veteran, Jon Voight. Both won Academy Awards for their performances.

United Artists

ESCAPISM

Courtesy, Amblin Entertainment

The mystery of UFOs and the longing for a sweeping solution to human problems were exploited in the 1978 film "Close Encounters of the Third Kind." Among others of a mysteriously chosen group of ordinary people, Richard Dreyfuss felt compelled to build a model of Devil's Tower, Wyoming, before being drawn to discover a secret base there and share in the first contact with superior, extraterrestrial beings.

Adults and children alike responded to the spectacular nonstop adventure crises in "Raiders of the Lost Ark," released in 1981. Situations, characters, and plot devices common to old multichapter Saturday afternoon serials were combined in a feature-length film that masked its melodramatic absurdities with fast-paced action and a tongue-in-cheek attitude toward itself. Its popularity generated a sequel, "Indiana Jones and the Temple of Doom," in 1984, which suggested that a kind of full-length serial might be developing.

10.

MILESTONES

Major events in the period 1968–1982 ranged from national tragedy, mindless murder, and religious fanaticism to human triumph and major advances for mankind. It was a time that saw the first man walk on the moon, and the first American—a woman—canonized as a Roman Catholic saint. It was also a time when we celebrated the nation's 200th birthday and discovered a renewed sense of patriotism and longing for peace. These and other events stand out in clear relief from the context of the longer-term, more complex developments and changes documented in the preceding nine chapters.

A tragedy of incalculable loss occurred at the very beginning of the period with the assassination of the Reverend Martin Luther King, Jr., whose doctrine of nonviolent resistance and peaceful civil disobedience of discriminatory laws had achieved major advances for black Americans and had made him the internationally respected leader of the civil rights movement. In the photograph *below*, Dr. King (center, in dark suit) leads a peaceful protest march from Selma, Alabama, where civil rights advocates were attacked by the police, to Montgomery, the state capital, to demand protection from the governor and the legislature.

Photo by Bruce Davidson, © 1968 Magnum Photos

AP/Wide World Photos

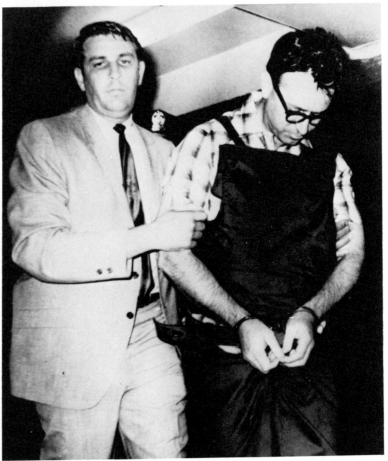

AP/Wide World Photos

ASSASSINATION AND AFTERMATH

The Reverend Martin Luther King, Jr., was killed on April 4, 1968, in Memphis, Tennessee. In a photograph (*opposite page, top*) taken the day before, he stood on the balcony of his motel in almost the same spot where he was shot. At his left is the Rev. Ralph Abernathy, who succeeded King as head of the Southern Christian Leadership Conference. At King's right is the Rev. Jesse Jackson, who emerged as the major black leader of the early 1980s and in 1984 became the first black American to seek the presidential nomination. King's assassin was James Earl Ray, who was returned to Memphis (*opposite page, bottom*) after an international manhunt and his seizure in London. It has never been revealed how Ray eluded immediate capture or where he got the funds and assistance that enabled him to flee the country.

Grief, despair, anguish, and rage were the reactions to King's death. Violent demonstrations in many cities led to arson, looting, and shootings. *Below,* soldiers with sheathed bayonets on their rifles patrol one of the worst-hit areas of Washington, D. C., three days after the assassination.

UPI/Bettmann

MURDERERS

The evil side of the drug-taking counterculture emerged with Charles Manson and the followers of his small cult. Convinced that civilization was being destroyed by black attacks, they lived in a desert commune and practiced strange rites and ceremonies. Manson and three cult members were convicted of the ritual murder of actress Sharon Tate and six companions, and were sentenced to death in the California gas chamber. Manson acted as his own attorney; he is seen here bringing papers to court during the 1970 trial.

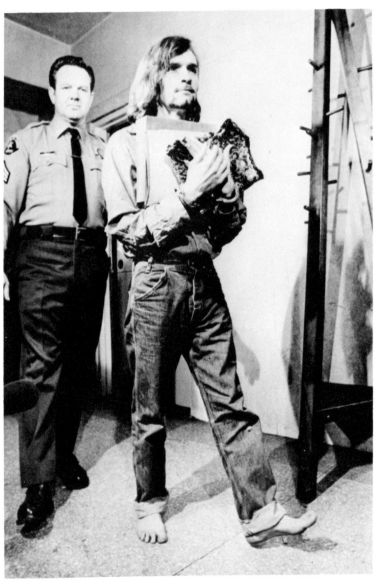

UPI/Bettmann

Multiple-murderer Gary Gilmore was executed by a firing squad in Utah, in January 1977. This was the first instance of capital punishment in the United States in ten years. It set off a storm of protest and a continuing debate between those favoring and those opposing the death penalty. It proved to be the first of a growing series of executions in the 1980s which appeals courts refused to countermand.

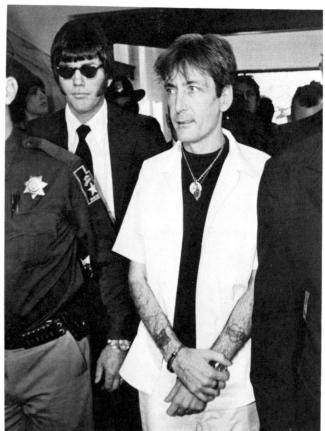

UPI/Bettmann

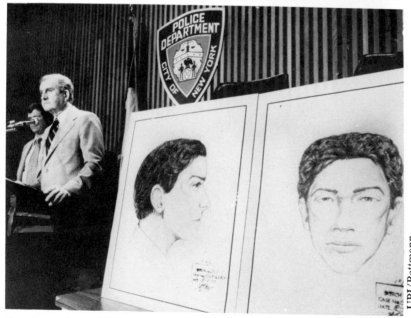

UPI/Bettmann

Letters signed "Son of Sam," sent to New York newspapers in 1976 and 1977, claimed credit for a series of shootings that killed six and wounded seven people in city and suburban neighborhoods. Near-hysterical fear grew until David R. Berkowitz, a mild postal clerk, was arrested as he was about to stage a shootout with automatic weapons in a dance hall. Berkowitz claimed to have received instructions from a local police dog; he was judged insane. Sketches displayed at a press conference during the investigation were based on fragmentary descriptions; they were a poor likeness of the killer.

RELIGION: INSANITY AND REVOLUTION

Jim Jones, leader of the People's Temple, ordered his followers to move to Guyana, where he established a religious dictatorship called Jonestown. In November 1978 a congressional group came to make inquiries on behalf of the relatives of some cult members. Paranoid, Jones had them killed, then ordered the colony to join him in suicide. Those who hesitated were shot; others, 911 in all, drank cyanide-laced fruit juice from tubs like the one in the photograph *below*.

Revolution forced the Shah of Iran to leave his country in January 1979. A few months later, followers of the Ayatollah Ruhollah Khomeini took control of the government and in November seized the American embassy in Teheran. Some ninety people were taken hostage, including sixty-five Americans. In the photograph (*opposite page, top*) militant Moslem students display photographs of blindfolded hostages as the Ayatollah looks on from a poster on the wall. Early negotiations and an abortive military rescue attempt failed, and the situation was a major factor in President Jimmy Carter's failure to win reelection. The hostages were released within hours of President Ronald Reagan's inauguration, January 1981, and were welcomed home with great joy, as in the New York City parade shown *opposite page, bottom*.

UPI/Bettmann

UPI/Bettmann

UPI/Bettmann

TROUBLE FROM OUTSIDE

AP/Wide World Photos

In May 1975, Cambodia seized the U.S. merchant ship *Mayaguez* and its crew of nineteen in disputed waters along its coast. In what some felt was overreaction, President Gerald Ford ordered military action to reclaim the ship. Thirty-eight Americans were killed. In the photograph, crew members wave as the freed ship comes into Singapore harbor.

Official U. S. Coast Guard Photo

A major mission of the United States Coast Guard along our Caribbean and Gulf coasts is to prevent smuggling. By far the greatest and most dangerous problem is the continual increase in drug traffic. Here, a Coast Guard boat brings in prisoners from the *Lukas M.*, which was intercepted carrying drugs in 1980.

DISASTERS OF MAN AND NATURE

Blackout. A man directs traffic at a New York City intersection after power grid failures throughout the northeast blacked out the city July 13, 1977. Overload measures instituted after the first such blackout twelve years earlier proved unequal to the demand for electricity in torrid midsummer.

UPI/Bettmann

AP/Wide World Photos

Earthquake. A Los Angeles couple camps out in their yard after a February 1971 quake has made their house unsafe. The day before, the husband had lost his job. "What else can happen?" he asked.

NATURAL FORCE

Mount St. Helens, in the State of Washington, became a devastatingly active volcano in 1980. After a minor eruption in March, it exploded violently on May 18, blowing 600 feet off its summit. Millions of cubic yards of earth and ash were thrown into the air and down the mountainside, and a wall of water was sent racing down the Toutle River valley. Vegetation was smothered in ash over hundreds of square miles. Property damage was enormous. More than fifty people were killed. Smaller, far less destructive eruptions occurred in the next two years.

UPI/Bettmann

UPI/Bettmann

The scene near Mount St. Helens after the major eruption gives some idea of what Pompeii and Herculaneum must have been like. Digging out took weeks in some places, up to a year in others. Close to the mountain, much land had to be abandoned to wait for nature to restore its growth and usefulness.

THE BOUNDLESS FRONTIER

Whatever excitement space achievements had generated in the twelve years since the U.S.S.R. had launched Sputnik, the first man-made, earth-orbiting satellite, nothing could equal the thrill of watching the first man on the moon. On July 20, 1969, between one-third and one-half of the human race watched live television transmission as Neil A. Armstrong stepped from the United States spaceship Apollo 11 to take the historic "one small step for a man, one giant leap for mankind." This photograph of his fellow crew member, Edwin E. Aldridge, Jr., was taken by Armstrong after they had planted the American flag. The light of the sun is extremely harsh because the moon has no atmosphere to modulate it. The wafflelike patterns in the moon's soil were produced by treads on the soles of the astronauts' footgear.

Courtesy, NASA

Courtesy, NASA

By the time of the fifth moon landing—the Apollo 16 mission in April 1972—equipment for traveling on the moon's surface and collecting additional samples of rock and soil was well developed. In these missions, a command module remained in orbit around the moon while two crew members piloted a lunar landing module, seen at the left, down to the surface. Here, John W. Young, commander of the landing mission, leaps in the moon's weak gravity as astronaut Charles M. Duke, Jr., the landing module pilot, takes his picture. The equipment in the distance is an ultraviolet camera and spectrograph.

This Apollo 16 mission photograph shows the Lunar Roving Vehicle—called the moon buggy by the astronauts—which permitted exploring a greater area and collecting heavier samples than was possible on foot.

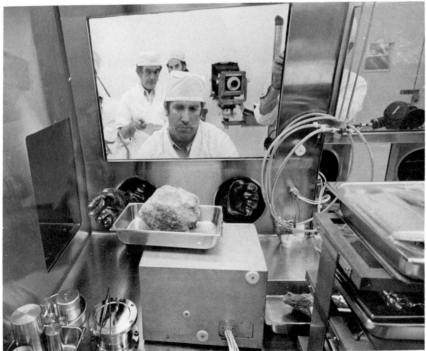

Lunar rocks and soil were brought back in sterile containers and examined in sterile, airless conditions to avoid contamination from the earth's atmosphere. Analysis of such samples has added greatly to knowledge of the history of the solar system as well as of the moon itself.

Courtesy, NASA

Skylab, the first American manned earth-orbit station, was launched in May 1973. Its function was to test equipment and the ability of personnel to stay in space for extended periods, do various kinds of work, and carry out scientific experiments. This picture, taken during the fourth Skylab mission, in February 1974, was made from the command and service module. The space station lacks one of its rectangular arrays of solar panels, which was lost during the original launching.

Courtesy, NASA, from U.S.S.R. Academy of Sciences

In July 1975, the United States and the U.S.S.R. undertook the first joint mission in space history. An American Apollo spacecraft and a Soviet Soyuz spacecraft were launched separately. They made rendezvous in space, coupled, and crews moved back and forth between the two craft to conduct joint experiments over a period of some forty-seven hours. Here is the Apollo spacecraft as photographed from Soyuz before the docking operation was begun.

Courtesy, NASA

The space shuttle is an airplane that is launched into orbit by rocket and can be piloted back to earth after a mission such as placing a communications satellite in orbit has been accomplished. Here, the first shuttle, the *United States*, is shown atop a carrier plane during testing in 1977. It was taken to a high altitude, then separated so its independent flight characteristics could be tested and analyzed. The controlled, soft landings on land possible with the shuttle are a great improvement over the parachute-into-ocean mode for recovering earlier American spacecraft.

In a 1979 triumph of the American space program, the unmanned Viking II landed on Mars and transmitted clear, detailed photographs of the terrain. The planet was revealed to be bleak, cold, dry, and nearly airless. There were no princesses, no Martians, no canals, and probably no life on Mars, much to the disappointment of science-fantasy fans.

1776–1976

The nation's biggest birthday party lasted all of its two-hundredth year and featured reenactments of our history as well as up-to-the-minute celebrations and events. On December 25, 1975, these enthusiasts recreated George Washington's most famous feat in the style commemorated by Emanuel Leutze's well-known painting. With a handful of troops, Washington crossed the Delaware River on Christmas night 1776 to make a surprise attack on Hessian troops hired by England who were stationed near Trenton, New Jersey. It was a turning point in the Revolutionary War.

UPI/Bettmann

UPI/Bettmann

A contrast in time occurs as this recreation of an early nineteenth-century Conestoga wagon train rolls through late twentieth-century Waterbury, Connecticut, to reenact a common sight at the beginning of national growth into the Midwest and beyond.

July Fourth is the day of our national birth. In the bicentennial year it came to a close as in every year, with fireworks. But in 1976, nothing matched the splendor or the emotional impact of the display at the Statue of Liberty, the internationally recognized symbol for all that is positive in America. This view, taken from New Jersey, contrasts the timeless character of the statue with the lighted towers of the World Trade Center in lower Manhattan.

AP/Wide World Photos

AP/Wide World Photos

A special feature of the Bicentennial celebration was Operation Sail, a flotilla of tall-masted sailing ships from all over the world that visited our major seaports. As they sailed through New York Harbor on July 4, 1976, they were vastly outnumbered by modern pleasure craft and Navy and Coast Guard vessels, but the symbolic message—that this was the way our first settlers arrived—was not lost.

FAITH AND PEACE

An American's religious dedication to mankind was recognized in
September 1975 when Mother Elizabeth Ann Seton was canonized a
saint in the Roman Catholic Church. Born in America in 1774, two
years before the United States was formed, she was converted to
Catholicism and established the American Sisters of Charity before her
death in 1821. The first American-born saint, she is represented in the
tapestry at the top of the photograph, which was hung in Saint Peter's
Square in the Vatican City, Rome. Pope Paul VI, with two priests, is
seen at the bottom of the picture as he conducts the canonization
ceremony.

UPI/Bettmann

UPI/Bettmann

A patriotism reawakened by the Bicentennial celebration and succeeding events was accompanied by an increasing desire for peace and opposition to the development and use of nuclear weapons. On June 13, 1982, hundreds of thousands of people jammed Central Park in New York City in the largest peace demonstration ever staged in America.

INDEX

A

C

T

X

Y

Z